Secrets of *Successful* Muslim Couples

MARRIAGE TIPS FOR A LIFETIME

NAIELAH ACKBARALI

Secrets of Successful Muslim Couples:
Marriage Tips for a Lifetime

Author Email: help@muslimacoaching.com

ISBN: 978-1-7395999-4-2 *Paperback*

Published in England by
Inspired Muslim Women Ltd
Romford, United Kingdom
Tel: +44 7 915 765 815
Email: info@inspiredmuslimwomen.com
Website: www.inspiredmuslimwomen.com

British Library Cataloguing in Publication Data.
A catalogue record for this book is also available from the British Library.

بسم الله الرحمن الرحيم

To every couple and spouse
who shared their lives with me,
thank you for teaching me.

Transliteration Table

ARABIC LETTER	ENGLISH TRANSLITERATION	ARABIC LETTER	ENGLISH TRANSLITERATION
ء	ʾ	ض	ḍ
ا	a, ā	ط	ṭ
ب	b	ظ	ẓ
ت	t	ع	ʿ, ʿa, ʿi, ʿu
ث	th	غ	gh
ج	j	ف	f
ح	ḥ	ق	q
خ	kh	ك	k
د	d	ل	l
ذ	dh	م	m
ر	r	ن	n
ز	z	و	w, ū, u
س	s	ه	h
ش	sh	ي	y, ī, i
ص	ṣ		

ARABIC SYMBOL	ENGLISH TRANSLITERATION	ENGLISH TRANSLATION
ﷺ	*ṣalla ʾLlāhu ʿalayhi wa sallam*	Allāh bless him and give him peace.
عليه السلام	*ʿalahī as-salām*	Peace be upon him.
رضي الله عنهم	*raḍiya ʾLlāhu ʿanhum*	May Allāh be pleased with them.
رضي الله عنها	*raḍiya ʾLlāhu ʿanhā*	May Allāh be pleased with her.
رضي الله عنه	*raḍiya ʾLlāhu ʿanhu*	May Allāh be pleased with him.

TABLE OF CONTENTS

Disclaimer: *The advice in this book is not suitable for anyone in a physically or emotionally abusive relationship. It is also not a replacement for professional psychotherapy or medical treatment.*

هُنَّ لِبَاسٌ لَّكُمْ
وَأَنتُمْ لِبَاسٌ لَّهُنَّ

They are a garment for you,
and you are a garment for them.

(*al-Baqara*, 2:187)

INTRODUCTION

GARMENTS FOR EACH OTHER

Out of every analogy ever created, the Qur'ān gives the most accurate description of what a loving marriage should look like. Allāh Most High beautifully compares spouses as garments for each other.

Allāh says:

> **"They are a garment for you, and you are a garment for them."**

(*al-Baqara*, 2:187)

A garment is worn for many reasons:

- It protects the body from the heat and cold.
- It covers a person's blemishes and faults.
- It adorns the person with its unique beauty.
- It holds tightly against the skin for extra support, and it fits in the most perfect of ways.

Similarly this is what a spouse is to a spouse.

- A spouse protects you from sinful lusts by fulfilling your needs of love.
- A spouse covers your weaknesses by forgiving and overlooking.
- A spouse adorns your life by decorating it with their beautiful Islamic character.
- A spouse is a source of support, security, warmth, and comfort through the ups and downs experienced in this world.

Thus, when spouses are garments for each other, they will feel safe and supported in each other's arms, and they will feel bare and exposed without the other person by their side.

But a garment only stays in good condition for as long as you look after it. Without proper care and attention, it is possible that what was once shiny and new can turn into something worn and torn. Most certainly, the same concept applies to a marriage.

After the initial excitement of getting married quiets down, reality kicks in for every couple. The newness of 'feeling' in love is replaced with the challenge of 'living' real love together. Some couples acquire these skills more quickly than others, but almost everyone undergoes a learning curve.

The truth is that many Muslim couples struggle with how to make their marriages successful at different points in their relationship. So, do not feel ashamed about your current marital situation or compare it to what you see on social media. You are most likely going through what other couples encounter behind closed doors: ups and downs, arguments, misunderstandings, and doubt.

The newness of 'feeling' in love is replaced with the challenge of 'living' real love together. Some couples acquire these skills more quickly than others, but almost everyone undergoes a learning curve.

Experts note that there are commonly four main stages to marriage:

1 **The Newlywed Phase:** You think you have found the one. Nothing else matters except being with your beloved. Your work, family, friends, and hobbies are put on the backburner. Your mind is consumed with how to please your spouse and make them the happiest person on the earth. You easily overlook their quirks and faults.

2 **The Noticing Faults Phase:** You slowly start to remove your rose-colored glasses and realize that your spouse is not as perfect as you thought. You find yourself getting irritated at your spouse's mistakes, but you continue to persevere in hopeful spirits.

3 **The Uncertainty Phase:** Your spouse is part of the problem. If they would stop doing x, y, and z, your marriage would be perfect. Your spouse has a hard time accepting your ideas of what will make things work. They may become resistant to change and you may become resistant to being more patient with their faults. Couples can experience doubts about their relationship during this stage. Some may seek third party support, while others may decide to end the union.

4 **The Friendship Phase:** You accept and respect your spouse for who they are, even if you do not agree with everything they do. You laugh when reminiscing about your marriage stories over the years. You smile at each other's quirks. You feel comfortable in their presence. You are happy to be their spouse. You still get irritated at their annoying habits, and you may find yourselves in a squabble every now and again. But those moments are a drop in the sea of your loving bond.

After over a decade of marriage coaching experience, what I have discovered is that successful Muslim couples also go through these four phases. So what separates successful Muslim couples from the rest?

Through rain and shine, they consciously and consistently invest their energy towards improving their marital bond.

In fact, it is not one specific thing that makes their marriage good, but it is a compilation of different components that helps the couple stay connected. I call this the Successful Muslim Couples Paradigm™.

The **Successful Muslim Couples Paradigm**™ consists of having a heart connection, an emotional connection, a physical connection, and a spiritual connection.

The Successful Muslim Couples Paradigm™

Heart Connection
Be devoted soulmates.

Emotional Connection
Be lifelong companions.

Physical Connection
Be passionate lovers.

Spiritual Connection
Be spiritual partners.

When these four components are present in a marriage and at optimal levels of strength, the couple can survive almost anything that tests their relationship.

However, when any of these components are missing or low on fuel, the marital bond will suffer until whatever is lacking is fulfilled or restored.

Take a moment to reflect about your own marriage. Are you happy with your relationship? Are you looking for ways to make your marriage better?

This book will help you to identify which areas of your marriage need work, and it will provide simple exercises of how to strengthen your marital bond.

It will also give you insight into which things could be hurting your marriage and solutions for how to turn your relationship around.

I have included real stories wherever relevant, although the names have been changed to protect each person's privacy.

If you are both on board, read this book together as a couple and complete the exercises. You can read a new chapter each week or space out the readings and exercises at your convenience.

If your spouse is not initially interested, do not lose hope; you can still make a difference. Read this book by yourself and gradually introduce the tips and exercises into your marriage.

I pray that these marriage tips are a means to improving and enhancing your relationship by providing helpful ideas and outlets for change. My intention is to help Muslim couples gain a better understanding of what it takes to maintain a successful marriage and how to be lifetime garments for each other.

PART 1

HEART CONNECTION

A heart connection is one of the deepest connections that spouses can have with each other. It is to know your spouse at a heart level by admiring the values that make up their core, being aware of their expectations for love, and caring about their concerns.

HEART
CONNECTION

COUPLES QUIZ

Take this quiz to discover the strength of your heart connection. For every statement that you agree with, give yourselves a point. Read about your score afterwards and the marriage tips that follow.

- [ ] We spend regular quality time together and find it enjoyable.
- [ ] We both feel like a high priority to the other person.
- [ ] We both believe our good times outweigh our bad times.
- [ ] We know each other's most important values, biggest dreams, and greatest goals.
- [ ] We know what true love means to each other.
- [ ] We have found ways to meet each other's most important needs for love.
- [ ] We try to address each other's most serious complaints and do not dismiss or ignore them.
- [ ] We can respectfully discuss major issues in our relationship without it turning into a fight.
- [ ] When one of us gets upset, the other knows how to be helpful.
- [ ] We make up with each other relatively quickly after any conflict.

Scores

9 to 10

Māshā'Allāh you have worked hard to become soulmates. Keep up whatever you are doing to maintain this sacred connection and cherish the rare blessing that Allāh has given you.

6 to 8

AlḥamduliLlāh you are trying to be good spouses and that is what matters. You may be experiencing trouble in certain areas, but once you work on improving your relationship, you will be connected at a deeper level. Follow the tips in the upcoming chapters to get started on your journey.

Below 5

Your heart connection needs some work. However, do not get discouraged by your score because it is possible to improve things. Try to complete the exercises in the upcoming chapters and see if practicing the advice makes a difference *insha'Allāh*.

Reflections

SECRET #1

BE PRESENT

Ahmad and Amina met in their late teens. They had never spoken to each other before but were introduced through mutual acquaintances.

Even though they were both young, inexperienced about life, and still in university, they decided to get married to follow the Sunna.

Their relationship started off blissfully. It was easy to make each other happy and forming a good marriage seemed effortless.

Yet as the years passed, the challenges came into their lives like crashing waves that weighed down on their marital bond.

They soon had a few kids – with a miscarriage in between – and spent less time with each other. Ahmad changed his jobs several times, and the family was forced to relocate to different places at various stages in their marriage.

As each year passed, they faced a new drama. Whether it was money problems, in-law issues, or parenting challenges, they were tested as a couple.

There were disagreements, misunderstandings, and hurt feelings, but they were overpowered by countless happy moments, uncontrollable laughs, and sweet tenderness. After over twenty-five years of marriage, they are still happily married.

Ahmad and Amina's marriage did not survive because it was rooted in passionate love. Their bond was not based on money or luxuries. Their relationship was not hanging on a thread for merely their children's sake. Simply put, their marriage was successful because they became good friends.

They intentionally chose to be there for each other through the ups-and-downs. They willfully demonstrated care and concern for each other despite the stormy weather. They deliberately picked up on each other's slack during moments of uncertainty.

Perhaps one of the reasons that you decided to marry your spouse was because of your deep need to feel loved by someone special. It is from your natural disposition (*fitra*) that you long for someone to care for you and accept you for who you are. Your spouse also shares the same wishes. They greatly crave your attention, support, and tenderness too.

Allāh Most High says:

> **"And among His signs is that He created for you mates from amongst yourselves so that you may dwell in tranquility with them, and He has put love and mercy between your hearts. Verily in that are signs for those who reflect."**

(*al-Rūm*, 30:21)

If you ponder over this verse, you will notice that Allāh Most High says that He created spouses for the purpose of the two people living together in tranquility.

Revelation is informing you that marriage is meant to be bliss and blessing – something that brings joy and peace into your life – as it is a means for tremendous spiritual good.

The secret behind achieving this sacred atmosphere is mentioned in the verse too. By constantly showing love and mercy towards one another, you both create a haven for yourselves and your children; a place where you always feel protected and secure from any outside evil.

Thus, if you want to make your marriage a lasting serene abode, you must live up to the Quranic principles of love and mercy. True love is not an 'idea' that you study, and it is not a 'feeling' that comes in the heat of the moment.

True love is a conscious decision, a behavior, a practice, and a constant contribution. True love is an opening for self-discovery, growth, and improvement. True love is a shared vision that you work towards every day.

Be Present In Body

Successful Muslim Couples are lifelong companions. They are there for each other through the thick and thin. They comfort each other during the hard times and appreciate each other during the good times. They ease each other's worries and celebrate each other's triumphs.

However, none of these things are possible if you are not physically present in the first place. Your spouse cannot hug themselves. Your spouse cannot hold their own hands. Your spouse cannot laugh at their own jokes.

For a marriage to thrive and survive, you need to be there for your spouse. You need to spend time with them. You need to show up.

Allāh Most High says:

> **"He is the One Who created you from a single soul, then from it made its spouse so he may find comfort in her."**

(*al- Aʿrāf*; 7:189)

You were once single, unmarried, and alone. Through Allāh's infinite blessings, He created a companion for you. Someone who has the potential to comfort you, care for you, and love you.

A common mistake that couples make is they stop dedicating time towards their marriage. Once the excitement of finding a spouse calms down, they return to their normal routines like when they were single.

They may initially try to balance their goals, ambitions, and career with their marriage. But when that becomes too difficult to manage, they put their relationship on the backburner to achieve worldly pursuits.

However, if you spend less time with your spouse, you run the risk of getting disconnected. As the days pass, you lose familiarity with who your spouse is and why you liked them in the first place.

When disagreements break out, you are less likely to overcome them gracefully because your friendship is not solid. Lifelong friendships require consistent commitment.

Even from the example of the Prophet ﷺ, you learn that downtime with your spouse is important. He ﷺ would visit his wives daily after *ʿAṣr* and find repose with the wife whose turn it was for that day. (*Bukhārī*, 5268)

He ﷺ talked and laughed with his wives. It is reported that he ﷺ playfully raced the Mother of the Believers ʿĀʾisha رضي الله عنها, even in the later years of their marriage. (*Abū Dāwūd*, 2578)

Successful Muslim Couples prioritize spending time with each other. They commit themselves to daily check-ins that can even be as short as twenty to thirty minutes. Whenever possible, they try to organize a weekly date night without their children, travel together, and organize family outings.

The Prophet ﷺ said, "All idle pastimes that a Muslim man engages in are falsehood, except for the shooting of his bow, the training of his horse, and his playing with his wife, for they are from the truth." (*Tirmidhī*, 1637) Every sweet second you spend with your spouse is worship for Allāh's sake.

Be Present In Mind

However, these couples are not just physically together; they are mentally together. When they spend time, Successful Muslim Couples give their undivided attention to each other and treat each other like friends.

Sitting in the same room while you scroll through your phones is not sufficient. Otherwise, your spouse is no different than a stranger at a bus stop. If you want to tighten your bond, you need to interact with each other, engage in conversation, laugh, and create happy memories.

Successful Muslim Couples agree on how to reduce distractions during their quality time. Whether it be ignoring their phones, turning off the television, or talking in the early morning while their kids are sleeping, they set up an environment that ensures the main spotlight is on them.

> Khadija and Omar were parents of several small children. At the beginning of their marriage, it was easy to enjoy quiet moments together. After having kids and tending to their needs throughout the day, Khadija was exhausted by the time Omar came home.
>
> Even though they were together and spending time like a happy family, she realized that she could not focus on what Omar was saying. Whenever the children were around, her attention was naturally drawn to their concerns and what they wanted.
>
> Khadija decided that it was best to save their alone time as a couple until after the children went to bed; this way her mind would be more receptive to what her husband talked about. Thereafter, she felt closer to him.

Be Present In Heart

The biggest factor that separates Successful Muslim Couples from the rest is what they talk about when they are together. Like all couples, they speak about routine things like children and work, but that is not what makes their friendship strong.

Successful Muslim Couples go beyond surface level topics, and they dive deep. They intentionally check up on each other, cultivate common interests, and share their dreams together. They get to know each other again and again, never concluding that they have learned enough about the other person.

They ask questions caringly. They listen with curiosity. They respond tenderly. Despite the worries that may be hanging over their shoulders, their hearts are present with each other.

If you want to create a similar atmosphere in your own marriage, you need to make the moves to share your lives together. You cannot claim to 'be married' if you do not put in effort to 'stay married.'

If you want to become soulmates and not just roommates, you must ask each other meaningful questions and care to hear the answers. You must remember the key points that were said and use that knowledge to understand who your spouse is as a person.

If you want to create a similar atmosphere in your own marriage, you need to make the moves to share your lives together. You cannot claim to 'be married' if you do not put in effort to 'stay married.'

When you give your spouse the space to express themselves and show your respect for their responses, a special trust is built between your hearts. Soon you gain exclusive access to your spouse's inner world. No one knows certain things about your spouse except you, and that's what makes your bond special.

When the Prophet ﷺ was asked who the most beloved person was to him, his first response was his wife ʿĀʾisha ﷺ. (*Bukhārī*, 3662)

When the Prophet ﷺ was troubled after receiving the revelation in the Cave of Ḥirāʾ, he ﷺ first confided in his wife Khadīja ﷺ. (*Bukhārī*, 3)

When the Prophet ﷺ was disappointed at his Companions not following his orders at the Treaty of Ḥudaybiyyah, he first consulted his wife Umm Salama ﷺ. (*Bukhārī*, 2731)

The connection that spouses share together is sacred and unique. They should be able to trust each other, confide in each other, console each other, and advise each other in ways that they cannot do with anyone else.

Private Spouses

Some spouses are harder to get through to than others. You may ask them questions but they always give brief answers. This can become very frustrating and saddening to the spouse who wants to hold a deep discussion.

You need to first determine why your spouse is so private. Are they naturally a quiet person? Are they interested in the questions asked? Are they troubled? Are there trust issues?

By pinpointing the real issue, you will gain insight into how to help your spouse be more open with you.

Sometimes doing nice things or investing time in your spouse's same interests can indirectly encourage a person to speak more.

Otherwise, you may need to gently share your feelings and kindly ask if there is anything that you can do to make things different.

The connection that spouses share together is sacred and unique. They should be able to trust each other, confide in each other, console each other, and advise each other in ways that they cannot do with anyone else.

Successful Muslim Couples do what it takes to make their marriage prosper. They keep their friendship alive and make a good marriage their priority.

HEART CONNECTION

COUPLES EXERCISE

As time passes, it is common for spouses to normalize their interactions. Go beyond routine conversations and dive deep by getting to know your spouse at a heart level.

Together

Choose a day and time that suits both of you. Find a relaxing place free of disruptions to attempt this exercise.

- Ask your spouse any of the questions on the following page.

- Only one person should talk, while the other person listens.

For the spouse responding to the question:

- Do answer thoughtfully and from the heart.

  Allow your spouse to know who you are and what you stand for at this point in your life.

- Do not act irritated if your spouse is surprised at your answers.

  Focus on helping them learn what makes you a good person.

For the spouse listening to the answer:

- Do act interested, give your spouse time to respond, and look at your spouse while they speak.
- Do not put down your spouse's ideas or mock their responses.

Individually

After hearing what your spouse says, take some time to reflect on your conversation.

- Were you able to comfortably speak with your spouse? Why or why not?
- Did you learn anything new about your spouse? Did you like what you learned?
- Do you share similar interests, dreams, or goals? Which ones are different?

Be a Successful Muslim Couple

Share your lives together. Dedicate time to check in on each other daily and be friends.

Meaningful Questions

Starters

1. How are you? What's new?
2. How are things going with (*your job, school, etc*)?

Dive Deep

1. If you could achieve anything in life, what would it be?
2. If you could start up your own business, what would you do?
3. Of all your family members, who are you closest to and why?
4. What's your favorite childhood memory? What's your least favorite?
5. What were you like in high school? Did you like your teen years?
6. Were there any difficult situations in your life that shaped who you are today?
7. Who are your best friends? Why do you like their company?

8. Which Quranic verse or hadith do you find most inspiring? Why?

9. When was the last time you felt extremely excited? What was it about?

10. When was the last time you felt really sad? What was it about?

11. What do you value most at this point in your life? Why?

12. If you could invest a million dollars in a charitable cause, what would it be?

13. What things stress you out the most? Why?

14. What's the best gift you ever received? Why?

15. If you could meet anyone in the world from the past or present, who would it be?

16. If the internet shut down for one day, what would you do with your time?

17. Where do you see society heading? How does that make you feel?

18. What's the nicest thing anyone has ever done for you? What's the worst?

19. Does the life you live now look like the life you envisioned when you were growing up?

20. If you could change anything about your life, what would it be?

Reflections

SECRET #2

FULFILL CORE NEEDS

Everyone has expectations of their marriage. However, unrealistic expectations can negatively impact your marital bond.

They persuade you to remain unhappy, even if you are in a promising relationship with a good person. Put your personal desires aside and first get clear on what marriage really is and what it is not.

Marriage is not a dream vacation.

Marriage is not about taking a luxurious holiday or nonstop adventure. Spouses who fall into this fantasy easily become bored with their spouses.

They start doubting the potential of their marriages too quickly because it is not as 'exciting' as it used to be. They compare their marriages to what they see on social media and think that they are missing out on something.

The truth is that for most people, that's just what happens. The newlywed stage is but a stage, and couples subsequently settle back into their normal routines.

Creating enjoyable moments together takes a conscious effort thereafter, and the simpler they are, the more sustainable it will be to recreate them.

Successful Muslim Couples come to terms with the fact that marriage is not a teenager fling but a spiritual responsibility. They do not compare their marriages to others because no one knows what happens behind closed doors.

Instead, they understand that creating a good marriage is a decision that stems from their maturity and the hard work they put in to make it good.

Marriage is not a cure for unhappiness.

Your spouse cannot make you happy, they can only make you happ*ier*. If you are expecting your spouse to continuously converse with you and spend every free moment with you, you could be putting more pressure on your relationship than it can bear.

Your spouse has their own problems and responsibilities outside of your relationship. Be considerate of their circumstances. They can only give you a certain amount of time and emotional energy before they run empty on gas.

When you married your spouse, you also married their family, their previous life, and their problems. Likewise, your spouse married your family, your previous life, and your problems. Creating harmony thereafter will always bring its unique challenges.

Rather than relying on them to make you feel whole, heal any open wounds with a qualified professional. Empower yourself by finding peace within yourself.

Marriage is not about being the same.

Your spouse does not need to become exactly like you for your marriage to succeed. Successful Muslim Couples are often very different from each other. However, they appreciate their unique differences and consider the variety in styles a plus for their relationship.

Give your spouse the space to be themselves. If you exert your effort towards trying to change your spouse into what you want, you will most likely push your spouse away or make your spouse resentful at your attempts. Base your expectations on who your spouse really is and not who you think your spouse should be.

Abdullah was a highflyer. He was rich, smart, witty, and determined to succeed in life. His wife, Safa, was a clerk at a local firm. She was diligent, caring, and a great people person. Abdullah was very attracted to her warm qualities.

Considering their situation, Abdullah thought Safa could do better with her career. He first suggested that she return to school and strive for a higher degree. Safa was not interested in being a student again. She questioned Abdullah's idea and rejected it.

As the years passed, Abdullah made it his mission to convince Safa how much she could potentially earn more, improve her skills, and be in a better position if she dedicated herself towards developing her qualifications. In return, Safa would get offended and turn her nose up at his idea. Every time he brought up the subject, her resentment towards her husband grew exponentially.

Abdullah finally realized that there was no point in trying to push her towards something she did not want. He eventually gave up on the idea. Even though he thought he was helping his wife, it hurt their relationship. Safa was not passionate about achieving in her career the same way Abdullah was. Her successes were in her relationships with people.

Realistic Expectations

Realistic expectations are relationship 'wants' that are reasonable and sensible. When your marriage is characterized by realistic expectations, it is easy for both spouses to succeed in the relationship.

Realistic expectations have two defining features. Firstly, they are attainable by most people and are not a rare occurrence amongst couples. Secondly, they are sustainable in the long run and do not involve immense effort to maintain.

A few examples are:

- Mutual trust in each other.
- Equal commitment to the relationship.
- Spoken appreciation and encouragement.
- Empathy towards experiences and emotions.
- Friendship and admiration for each other.
- Satisfying sexual experiences.
- Mutual understanding and compromise.
- Respect for differences and boundaries.
- Spending regular quality time together.
- Shared acts of kindness and generosity.

Core Needs For Love

Core needs for love are relationship expectations that must be fulfilled for your spouse to be happy. Unlike other expectations, they are usually non-negotiable.

Out of all your spouse's wishes and desires, core needs are the most important needs to fulfill on a consistent basis – even if you are going through a testing time. When core needs are left unmet, your spouse will grow unhappy and question the state of the marriage.

Just like every person in this world has a unique personality, every spouse will have unique needs for love. Even if a couple is connected at the hip, each person will differ on how to interpret what love means to them.

For example, your spouse may need to hear loving words of endearment every day, while you may need regular physical touch.

If you do not compliment your spouse daily, they will feel unloved. Similarly, if your spouse does not show you enough affection, you will feel unsatisfied.

Just like every person in this world has a unique personality, every spouse will have unique needs for love. Even if a couple is connected at the hip, each person will differ on how to interpret what love means to them.

Both of you need love, but what you each decipher to be love is different. A marriage thrives when both spouses' needs for love are prioritized and fulfilled, and it falls apart when they are neglected and ignored.

There are a few ways to figure out your spouse's core needs:

- Openly ask them.
- Take note of what they regularly request from you.
- Pay attention to what disappoints them.

For many, core needs become apparent during conflict.

> Qasim and Maria were married for over fifteen years and had several children of varying ages. Qasim worked abroad but would visit the family every few months. During his trips, he would try to spend as much time as he could with his children and make up for the lost time.
>
> Maria was a stay-at-home mother who dedicated herself to raising their children. She was often pulled in several directions, which greatly stressed her out. Even though she was happy for Qasim to visit and lend a helping hand, it was difficult to balance his needs with the children's needs.
>
> On a few occasions Maria was moody and mean to Qasim. Qasim could not make sense of Maria's behavior. He felt unappreciated and overwhelmed with his duty to financially support the family. He was growing unhappy with his marriage.
>
> One day Maria was in a better mood and spoke to Qasim in a loving manner. Qasim let out a sigh of relief and said, "That's better." Maria asked him what he meant. Qasim explained that he needed her to be cheerful when he was around. He wanted to hear her positivity and gratitude for his sacrifices.

Do not expect your spouse to read your mind and know what you want. You must teach your spouse how to love you by openly communicating your needs, wants, and desires.

It may be the case that your spouse is aware of your core needs, but they do not fulfill them consistently. Find out why, but without accusing them of being a bad spouse or implying it. Perhaps your spouse needs a gentle reminder more often, or they do not truly realize that you feel unloved.

Do not expect your spouse to read your mind and know what you want. You must teach your spouse how to love you by openly communicating your needs, wants, and desires.

Successful Muslim Couples are in tune with each other's needs. They understand what it takes to make their spouse feel loved and show love based on that definition.

HEART CONNECTION

COUPLES EXERCISE

Share your ideas about what love means. Get in touch with each other's core needs and do what it takes to fulfill them.

Together

Choose a day and time that suits both of you. Find a relaxing place free of disruptions to attempt this exercise.

- Ask your spouse:
  - "What makes you feel loved?"
  - "What are your three most important needs?"
  - "Do you need that on a daily, weekly, or monthly basis? How will you feel if I do not fulfill them?"
- Only one person should talk, while the other person listens.

For the spouse responding to the question:

- Do answer honestly and from the heart.

  Help your spouse understand what you are hoping for in a marital bond.

- Do not sneak in comments that point towards the things that your spouse is not doing.

  For example, "Love means that your spouse helps with the household chores, which you never do."

For the spouse listening to the answer:

- Do act interested, give your spouse time to respond, and look at your spouse while they speak.
- Do not roll your eyes, get frustrated at your spouse's delay in responding, or put down their ideas.

  Remain patient and give them the space to think.

Individually

After hearing what your spouse says, take some time to reflect about where you both match up in your ideals.

- Are you comfortable with your spouse's vision of what love is? Why or why not?
- Do you share the same expectations? Which ones are different?
- Are you willing to fulfill all your spouse's core needs for love? Why or why not?

Be a Successful Muslim Couple

Renew your commitment to your marriage. Intend to show love to your spouse as best as you can.

Reflections

SECRET #3

HEED COMPLAINTS

Every spouse complains. Fundamentally, a complaint is a popup message alerting you that your spouse is dissatisfied with something. It could be about your behavior, the relationship, or their in-laws.

Complaining can occur for various reasons and over different issues. Complaints can be about something major, minor, urgent, unimportant, serious, or silly – which is why slipping into the habit of ignoring complaints is all too easy to do.

However, some complaints are weightier than others, and disregarding them could cost your entire relationship with your spouse. In principle, if serious complaints are addressed sooner than later, it prevents bigger problems from occurring.

Through trial and error, Successful Muslim Couples master the skill of reading their spouses. They know when they must give their spouse's complaints their undivided attention and when they can casually overlook what was said. The Prophet ﷺ also took note of when his wives were upset at him.

The Mother of the Believers ʿĀʾisha رضي الله عنها reported that the Messenger of Allāh ﷺ said, "Indeed, I can tell when you are angry or pleased with me." I said, "How do you know that, O Messenger of Allāh?" The Prophet ﷺ said, "Verily, when you are pleased, you say: Yes, by the Lord of Muḥammad! But when we you are upset, you say: No, by the Lord of Ibrāhīm!" I said, "Yes, but I only leave your name (and I do not stop loving you)." (*Bukhārī*, 6078)

Making the Distinction

Serious complaints are normally rooted in unmet needs or unmarked boundaries. Essentially, your spouse believes that they are not getting what they want out of the relationship or they are being pushed beyond limits. Indeed, underneath every complaint is a cry for change.

It is as if your spouse is saying, "I am not happy! I want things to be different! Please help!" Even though it may sound like, "You never consider my feelings!" or "You don't understand!" or "You always forget!"

When your spouse complains, take note of the following:

- **The intensity of their reaction:** Are they making a big deal over what happened? Or did things blow over after a few minutes?
- **The words expressed:** Are they informing you that they are very angry, disappointed, hurt, or frustrated? Or are they slightly annoyed, upset, offended, or irritated?
- **The tone of voice:** Are they yelling and shouting? Or is their voice at a normal pitch?
- **The body language used:** Are they crying from upset? Is their face red hot with rage? Are they scowling in anger? Are their arms crossed in frustration? Or is their body language inviting?
- **The aftereffects:** Are they cold and withdrawn? Or are they acting like usual?
- **The frequency:** Does the issue keep coming up? Or is it a one-off occurrence?

If your spouse's complaints elicit a response that stands out from the rest, then that is a complaint that you do not want to ignore. This may seem like common sense, but it is surprising how regularly spouses tune each other out or dismiss complaints.

Common complaints between spouses are feeling disrespected, undermined, controlled, misunderstood, unappreciated, nagged, unsafe, overworked, sexually dissatisfied, or insecure.

The implicit message could be a need for more respect, admiration, trust, acceptance, appreciation, attention, security, commitment, consideration, intimacy, affection, loyalty, or transparency.

When unmet needs remain unfulfilled or boundaries keep being crossed, major fights will break out.

If your spouse's complaints are continuously ignored, dismissed, or minimized, resentment will build and grudges will invade their heart. This only intensifies the issue at hand and makes it more difficult to resolve.

Dealing With Complaints

No one likes to feel like the bad guy in the relationship. When your spouse complains, it is natural that you will feel criticized, attacked, or targeted. You may even question the validity of their statements and instinctively want to fight back.

Successful Muslim Couples often rely on these tips:

1. Calm Down: Try to avoid taking what your spouse says personally. View their complaint as a means to improve your relationship and as a way to draw nearer to Allāh Most High. This will only increase you in goodness and reward.

2. Listen: Focus on the idea that someone you care about is hurting. Open your ears and your heart to what is being said. Turn towards your spouse, look them in the eyes, and listen with attentiveness. Try to understand the message. What is your spouse communicating to you? What do they want from you? What is the missing need? Get clear on the real issue.

Even if the complaint aggravates your nerves, be patient and refrain from lashing out. If you are too impulsive, you may create bigger conflict, which is not what you want.

3. Empathize: Before responding with what you think, it helps to empathize with your spouse's feelings. Empathizing is different from agreeing. You are not admitting that what your spouse said is correct.

Rather, empathizing means that if you were to put yourself in your spouse's shoes, you would understand why they feel the way they do. This increases your concern for them.

4. Validate: Validating your spouse's feelings can quickly reduce heightened tension. Simple phrases can go a long way, like "I understand what you are saying," or "I hear that you are upset, and I want us to find a solution."

Even a nod or an "uh-huh" can work wonders. Show your spouse that you care, and comfort them before challenging their beliefs.

5. Apologize: Whenever you decide to respond, be smart about it. Your spouse is complaining for a reason. It does not make sense to deny what they said or invent flaky excuses.

Admit any wrong and soothe misunderstandings. Speak gently, slowly, and cautiously. It will help your spouse to be more open to your solutions.

6. Compromise: Be positive and solution oriented. Share your ideas for what you think could make the situation better. Offer to help and be flexible in whatever way you can.

It is quite possible that you will not initially agree on a solution. Do not try to force it. Suggest what you think could work, and request that your spouse thinks about it.

Give your spouse the space to consider all options. Agree on a day and time to return to the conversation.

Try to see eye-to-eye and reach common ground. Learn to think as a couple and settle for what is best for your relationship, not just yourself.

Despite having the authoritative position of being a messenger of God, the Prophet ﷺ consulted his wives رضي الله عنهن on various occasions and listened to their opinions. He ﷺ even took the advice of Umm Salama رضي الله عنها during the Treaty of Ḥudaybiyyah, which resulted in the unification of the Muslims.

Based on their own experience and intelligence, your spouse may have good suggestions that you could benefit from. Be open to hearing their input and experimenting with their ideas.

Even if you do not fully agree with them, think of the bigger picture of having a happy marriage.

Sometimes, tension can be subdued in minutes by sending the signal that you are willing to compromise.

> Hamza and Layla had only been married for two years. They were dedicated to making each other happy but Layla sometimes felt micromanaged by Hamza.
>
> Whenever she wanted to organize things her way, he always seemed to have feedback on how it should be done differently.
>
> She would usually give in to his opinions, thinking that it would keep their marriage good. One day they

were deciding how to arrange the household furniture for their new apartment.

Layla had already planned for the dresser to be placed in a certain spot, but when Hamza heard her idea, he innocently rejected it and asserted that another place would be better.

Layla snapped. She was through with putting up with his comments. "You are always telling me what to do!" she exclaimed.

Hamza was surprised at her response. "Every time I want something my way, you tell me how it should be different!" she cried out. Hamza quickly apologized and said, "Sorry I did not know that you felt that way."

Layla's nerves eased. She loved her husband, but she was annoyed at his behavior. She decided to explain to him how long this had been bothering her and what he could do to make things different.

Hamza listened to Layla speak and considered her point of view. Within a short period of time, they were acting like their usual selves as if nothing happened, and the dresser was placed where they both liked it.

Compromising is never a perfect solution. Neither person gets what they completely want, but no one completely loses either.

You do not need to get your way all the time to be happy. What matters is that you work together as a team to find a solution that settles your major concerns and restores your connection.

Switch your mindset from thinking of only 'me' to 'we.'

Conflict Protocol

1

Calm Down.

Take a break and cool the fire inside.

2

Listen.

Open your ears to the message.

3

Empathize.

Understand how your spouse feels.

4

Validate.

Say something that shows you care.

5

Apologize.

Take responsibility for any mistakes or wrongdoing.

6

Compromise.

Decide on what is best for your marriage.

Getting Defensive

Defensiveness is a common response to criticism. It is to divert the focus away from any criticism towards something else.

When a person is on the defensive, they may shift the blame onto their spouse, justify their questionable behavior, be defiant, lash out, or play victim. This only makes resolving complaints doubly difficult, and it causes arguments to run around in never-ending circles.

At its root, defensiveness is a protective mechanism. The defensive person tries to guard themselves from feeling emotions of anger, hurt, or shame. This may be due to a hidden fear of rejection, abandonment, humiliation, or failure.

1. Know yourself. If you notice that you are becoming overly defensive, agree with your spouse to stop discussing the issue, take a break, and resume talking about the topic later. You will not make any progress by continuing to talk about it.

2. Get clear on why the complaint is bothering you so much. Is it because of what your spouse is saying, how they are saying it, or something completely unrelated? Be fair in your assessment.

3. Tap into your inner self. What do you want from the situation? What is in the best interest for both of you? Once you know why you were reacting defensively and are now in control of your emotions, reintroduce the topic in a way that makes you feel comfortable.

4. Explain to your spouse what was going through your mind. Offer solutions for how they can state their complaints without triggering a defensive response from your end.

Hasan and Rahma were married for over ten years. Like any couple, they had their ups and downs but thankfully came out as a team in the end.

Hasan wanted to invest his savings in buying a house, but he could not afford a new property. He decided to purchase an older house and renovate it.

Rahma agreed to Hasan's plan. She was excited to become a homeowner. The two of them spent months house hunting and finally settled on a two-story house.

They spoke endlessly about what changes needed to be made and budgeted carefully. It was a very stressful situation, especially when the workers made careless mistakes.

After a few weeks of their renovation project, Rahma's nerves were shot and she grew in agitation at anyone's mistakes. Hasan was overwhelmed by Rahma's new attitude. She seemed to become bossier with each passing day, declaring that her way was better.

One day, Hasan was tidying the bathroom. When Rahma saw what he was doing, she became annoyed at his attempt. "That's not how you do it!" Rahma exclaimed.

Hasan's stress levels burst through the roof. He threw down his tool and stormed off. His face was boiling hot and his body burned with anger.

Rahma followed him into another room. "You keep telling me what to do!" he yelled over his shoulder. Rahma's eyes filled with tears.

Hasan turned around and continued shouting, "You want everything to be perfect! You blame me for everything! I am sick of it!"

Rahma grew quiet. She felt bad about complaining. Perhaps she was exaggerating. She apologized but Hasan would not calm down.

Rahma felt at a loss with how to handle his intense emotions. She left the room and cried harder.

Hasan tried to find his senses. He knew that his outburst was extreme, but he hated Rahma's insistence on things being her way. Once he felt in control of himself, he approached her.

As best as he could, he calmly said to her, "Sorry, I did not mean to make you cry, but I cannot stand it when you talk to me that way. I don't like to feel like I am not good at what I do. Just tell me what you want and I will make it happen. You don't have to criticize me."

Rahma realized that Hasan had a fair point. She was being insensitive to all the effort he had put in and how much he tried to cater to her desires. She apologized again and promised to be more careful with her words when saying what she wanted.

Sarcastic & Avoidant Spouses

Sometimes spouses can use sarcasm to communicate their complaints and annoyance. Whereas humor is needed in every marriage, resorting to sarcasm to convey unmet needs is risky. Your spouse could easily misinterpret what you mean and get very offended.

How can you tell the difference between innocent humor and cutting sarcasm?

When you tell a joke, both people find it funny. When you make an inappropriate sarcastic comment, you are the only one laughing, and most likely, your spouse is hurting.

Sarcasm is a type of indirect defensiveness. To the receiving spouse, it may seem subtle, less aggressive, and innocent. However, its underlying message is more disrespectful, inconsiderate, and nasty. A basic translation is, "You are the fool, not me." Sarcasm is contemptuous behavior that may stem from a lack of empathy.

Another type of indirect defensiveness is avoiding conflict altogether. Avoidant spouses convince themselves that they are doing a good deed by keeping quiet and running away from conflict. They may hurriedly leave the room, ignore their spouses, or disengage from deeper conversations.

The Prophet ﷺ said, "Do not hate each other, do not envy each other, do not turn away from each other, but rather be servants of Allāh as brothers." (*Bukhārī, 6065*)

Do not turn away from your spouse. The silent treatment is silent torture. It only hurts the situation more because your spouse often feels stuck and unaware of how to fix things.

When you avoid confrontation or sweep your problems under the rug, nothing changes. The relationship keeps moving but without both of you on board. You may pretend to be married, but beyond the surface, you are not a connected couple.

Because you do not take the means to air out the issues that bother you, a common side effect of avoidant behavior is that you become plagued with bad opinion of your spouse.

This only complicates matters. You notice that you feel angry at your spouse, but you cannot pinpoint the exact reason why.

The solution for sarcastic and avoidant spouses is that they must learn how to openly communicate their needs and stop hiding their vulnerable feelings.

Constant Complainers

Constant complainers are spouses who complain about almost anything and everything. It can be intentional or an oblivious bad habit. Either way, the spouse who is on the receiving end often feels helpless and frustrated.

If your spouse is a constant complainer, avoid falling into the trap of blaming yourself and allowing their comments to erode your confidence. Constant complainers usually have deeply rooted insecurities that have nothing to do with you.

On the other hand, your spouse may not know how much their complaining is affecting you. If that is the case, do not hide your feelings from them.

However, instead of angrily accusing them of constantly complaining, in a calm and composed manner let them know how you feel and ask for a solution. Responding with bad behavior to bad behavior will only result in a bad fight.

If your spouse has unresolved self-esteem issues, then they need to take personal responsibility for it and seek appropriate help. As a spouse, you cannot remedy their insecurities, but you can act as a support through their healing journey.

Reframing Complaints

It is easier to complain about something than to ask someone to help you. Complaining takes less thought, and it is cheered on by strong emotions of feeling wronged and deprived.

Successful Muslim Couples slip into complaining too, but they quickly change the way that they speak when complaining proves ineffective.

As an alternative, they first get clear on what they really want from their spouse, and then express their need respectfully.

Try this formula:

1. **Start Smart:** Calm down and introduce the topic in a dignified manner. Don't approach your spouse when your emotions are running wild. Crying and yelling can become frustrating when it is done frequently and without need.

2. **State A Specific Need:** Avoid bombarding your spouse with vague statements, like "You need to help more." Get specific. What would your spouse be doing if they did what you said? That is the crux of the matter.

3. **Say It With An 'I':** Reword your complaint. Drop the accusative 'you' and frame your need in the form of a specific request.

   For example, instead of saying "You never help around the house," politely ask your spouse to do a particular chore, like "On Friday, I would like you to dust the bookshelves. Is that possible?"

4. **Sweeten The Deal:** Invite your spouse to cater to your requests. You can increase your spouse's chance of responding positively by adding warm words of encouragement, such as "I would really appreciate your help please."

Choose a time when your spouse would be more receptive to hearing your request. For example, if your spouse is busy with writing an email, first double check that it is okay to speak to them.

If not, inquire about when it would be more convenient. This way you ensure that they are in a mindset to hear you and honor your wishes.

Take care to thank your spouse whenever they fulfill your request, even if it is not done exactly how you hoped. Focus on the beauty of your spouse's generosity rather than the ugliness of their faults.

Couples should also consider meeting on a weekly basis to openly discuss anything that is bothering them. Addressing issues sooner than later can prevent minor problems from snowballing into something bigger.

Be wary of complaining to family and friends about your spouse. It usually does more harm than good. You may cause unnecessary friction amongst others, or your family and friends may immediately take your side and influence you to grow in anger towards your spouse.

The Prophet ﷺ said:

> **"Whoever conceals the faults of a Muslim, Allāh will conceal his faults in this world and the Hereafter."**

(*Muslim*, 2699)

Successful Muslim Couples do not haphazardly expose their spouse's faults to others. Instead, they work towards resolving their complaints between each other or they seek third party support.

Making Up

The factor that makes Successful Muslim Couples stand out from the rest is the way that they repair after a dispute.

Instead of feeling distant from each other, Successful Muslim Couples feel closer. They give each other a hug. They hold each other's hands. They smile and laugh again. They may even go out for a treat to restore the connection.

Every couple has the potential to do the same. It requires that you sincerely focus on making your marriage a peaceful abode and not a place of lingering grudges.

If you find it difficult to make up with your spouse, then perhaps the issue was not dealt with completely or maybe you personally find it difficult to let go after someone hurts you.

A good marriage is built upon trial and error. You will each make different mistakes at different points in the relationship. But sometimes you learn more about each other through the hard times than during the good times.

Real marriages are not perfect, and perfect marriages are not real. Give your spouse another chance. Make the decision to clear your heart of ill feelings and replace it with the hope that your relationship will get better.

Successful Muslim Couples communicate their needs, boundaries, and wants to each other. They listen to each other with curiosity and open mindedness. They care about what the other person is saying and value their opinion, even if they do not agree.

HEART CONNECTION

COUPLES EXERCISE

Allow your spouse the chance to feel heard and understood. Work as a team to become aware of the real issues that are impacting your marriage.

Together

Choose a day and time that suits both of you. Find a relaxing place free of disruptions to attempt this exercise.

- Ask your spouse:
  - "Are you satisfied with the way we handle complaints in our marriage?"
  - "What needs to change for it to get better?"
  - "How often should we check up on each other's feelings and complaints?"
- Only one person should talk, while the other person listens.

For the spouse responding to the question:

- Do answer honestly and from the heart.

  Be gentle with your words and clear on what is bothering you.

- Do not accuse or insult your spouse.

  Focus on the greater goal of improving your marriage.

For the spouse listening to the answer:

- Do validate your spouse's opinions and look at your spouse while they speak.
- Do not get angry, defensive, or tell your spouse how to feel. Remain patient and open-minded.

Individually

After hearing what your spouse says, reflect on everything mentioned.

- Did you both agree on the same major issues? Why or why not?
- Were you able to listen to each other without it turning into a fight?
- Did you learn anything new about how your spouse feels?

Be a Successful Muslim Couple

Commit to openly listening to each other's complaints on a regular basis.

Reflections

PART 2

EMOTIONAL CONNECTION

An emotional connection encourages a lifelong companionship. When your spouse is your friend, you enjoy doing nice things for them, feel happy to be around them, and appreciate the gifts they bring to your life.

EMOTIONAL
CONNECTION

COUPLES QUIZ

Take this quiz to discover the strength of your emotional connection. For every statement that you agree with, give yourselves a point. Read about your score afterwards and the marriage tips that follow.

- [ ] We strive to demonstrate the best character with each other.
- [ ] We do not irrationally take out our anger on each other.
- [ ] We are open to changing our individual behavior if it is impacting our marital bond.
- [ ] We do not name call, insult, or negatively label each other.
- [ ] We practice patience and forgiveness with each other's faults and annoying habits.
- [ ] We understand each other's greater intentions and admire them.
- [ ] We use kind words when asking for favors.
- [ ] We admire each other's strengths.
- [ ] We frequently express gratitude and words of appreciation to each other.
- [ ] We do not feel underappreciated, nitpicked, or micromanaged.

Scores

9 to 10

Māshā'Allāh your friendship is solid. Continue to give back to each other and reap the benefits of your companionship.

6 to 8

You probably have happy moments in your marriage, but the way you treat each other can be improved. Gain better insight and ideas on how to become good friends with the tips that follow.

Below 5

Your emotional connection is on shaky grounds, but things can change for the better. Try to complete the exercises in the upcoming chapters and see if practicing the advice makes a difference *insha'Allāh*.

Reflections

SECRET #4

EXCEL IN THE SUNNA

Spouses often think that they need to return to the Islamic laws (*fiqh*) of marriage to know how to make their marriage successful. However, scholars usually explain that merely abiding by the *fiqh* rulings is not what will make your marriage good.

If you want the best recipe for marital success, then return to revelation and base your outlook on what the Qur'ān and Sunna say about how to behave as a believer.

The message from Allāh Most High and the Prophet ﷺ is almost always to strive beyond the bare minimum and excel in goodness.

Allāh Most High says:

> **"And do good, for Allāh certainly loves the good doers."**

(*al-Baqara*, 2:195)

Successful Muslim Couples strive to do good with each other. When one person does something nice, the other person feels compelled to return the favor.

Good deeds between spouses can happen in all types of shapes and sizes. From getting your spouse a glass of water when they are tired, to organizing a fun date night, to sacrificing your time to help. There are so many gates to goodness in a marriage, and no action is deemed insignificant.

In his own home, the Prophet ﷺ used to keep himself busy serving his family, and when it was time for the prayer, he would attend the prayer. (*Bukhārī*, 6039) He ﷺ would milk his sheep, patch his garment, serve himself, and mend his shoes.

Emulating Prophetic Character

The Prophet ﷺ said, "Verily, the most complete believers in faith are those who are the best in character and those who are the kindest to their families." (*Tirmidhī*, 2612)

According to the Prophet's noble words, all Muslims must demonstrate the strength of their faith by displaying good Islamic character. This especially holds true for spouses.

It is easy to let your guard down and stop caring about how you treat the people in your household. But it will catch up with you in the long run if you are not attentive.

Marriage is a friendship, and you cannot have a lifelong bond with someone without showing good character.

If you think about what attracts you to spending time with someone, it is not because you know that they pray all night or fast every day; it is dependent upon the way that they treat you.

Everyone is drawn to someone who is warm, giving, cheerful, forgiving, patient, considerate, and loving. Thus, a spouse who focuses on demonstrating good character frequently gets what they want out of their relationship.

The Prophet ﷺ said, "Nothing is heavier upon the scale of a believer on the Day of Resurrection than his good character. Verily, Allāh hates the vulgar and obscene." (*Tirmidhī*, 2002)

Demonstrating good character matters to Allāh Most High, and it should matter to you too. Allāh does not want you to act distastefully towards your spouse. He wants you to be the best believer that you can be.

The Prophet ﷺ said, "Verily a believer reaches the rank of someone who fasts all day and prays all night with his good character." (*Abū Dāwūd*, 4798)

Good character can be a means to increase in good deeds and enter you into Paradise. By treating your spouse nicely, you can attain the reward of a dedicated worshipper.

However, good character is not based upon your personal opinions and theories. If you want to know what good character is, then you must look at how the Prophet ﷺ treated people. He ﷺ is your role model of how to act and react in your marriage.

He ﷺ was known to be the most gentle, loving, and caring human being to ever walk the face of the earth; consequently, he ﷺ made everyone feel special.

He ﷺ was patient and kind, even when others were harsh with him.

He ﷺ would turn his body completely to face anyone who spoke to him, allowing them to feel important and heard, regardless of their social standing.

He ﷺ was generous with his time and wealth, which warmed the hearts of those around him.

He ﷺ was understanding of people's circumstances, even to the extent of shortening his own prayers for the sake of mothers with crying babies.

He ﷺ was accommodating to the concerns of others, avidly looking for ways to unite hearts and make his teachings easy to practice.

He ﷺ was easy to speak to and made himself available to the entire community, despite being a state leader, military commander, neighbor, husband, and father.

He ﷺ would tell jokes and make others smile.

He ﷺ is the true exemplar and guide of how Muslims need to interact with others. Most certainly, the blessings in a marriage come from following his ﷺ beautiful ways.

Controlling Anger

Being polite and amicable comes easily when you are in a good mood. The real test of character is how you treat others when you are angry, upset, and frustrated.

In a marriage, it is expected that you will get angry at your spouse. You are intimately living with another human being who may have living habits that are starkly different from your own. They may make choices that you do not respect. They may even disappoint you in the things that mean the most to you.

Occasionally blowing up and getting hotheaded can happen to even the best of people, but this should not be the norm.

The Prophet ﷺ also became angry at his wives رضي الله عنهن, but his anger was reserved. He ﷺ never hit a woman, child, or animal. He ﷺ did not use vulgar words or lie.

In one instance, out of her jealousy, the Mother of the Believers ʿĀʾisha رضي الله عنها made a distasteful remark about the Mother of the Believers Khadija رضي الله عنها.

The Prophet ﷺ became extremely angry to an intensity that Lady ʿĀʾisha رضي الله عنها had never seen before. His face turned red like when revelation descended. However, he ﷺ kept his composure and corrected Lady ʿĀʾisha رضي الله عنها by explaining how much Lady Khadija رضي الله عنها meant to him. (*Bukhārī*, 3821; *Muslim*, 2437; *Ṭabarānī*, 14)

The Prophet ﷺ said, "The strong person is not the one who can overpower others. Rather, the strong person is the one who controls himself when angry." (*Bukhārī*, 6114)

When your anger controls you, and you do not control it, it can be destructive and deceptive. In a fit of rage, the ego justifies its story based on facts that are often one-sided. This can cause you to get on the defensive too soon or too often.

Uncontrolled anger can also provoke you to yell, unduly ignore others, or shut down. Consequently, if you do not understand how to regulate your emotions in a productive manner, you could unjustly hurt those around you and haphazardly ruin your relationships with good people.

Do not expect your spouse to put up with your unreasonable behavior. The more you act disrespectfully, the more your spouse will lose their patience and their willingness to stay in the relationship. Instead of wounding your marital bond, take responsibility for your emotions, and find other ways to express them.

Allāh Most High says: "And whoever is mindful of Allāh, He will make their matters easy for them." (*aṭ-Ṭalāq*, 65:4) *Taqwā* means to be mindful of Allāh's presence. When you possess *taqwā*, you safeguard yourself from committing sins and actions that displease your Creator. You stay far away from Allāh's limits so that you are always striving to engage in what is pleasing to Allāh Most High.

At its core, having *taqwā* is about remembering that Allāh Most High sees and hears everything that you do, and you will be asked about it. If you focus on the fact that He sees you, your behavior will quickly change. People tend to act differently when they know that they are being watched.

Sunna Remedies for Anger

Seek refuge in Allāh.

The Prophet ﷺ said regarding an angry person:

"If he says: 'I seek refuge with Allāh from Satan.' then all his anger will go away."

(*Bukhārī*, 3282)

Change positions.

The Prophet ﷺ said:

"If one of you is angry while he is standing, let him sit down so his anger will leave him; otherwise, let him lie down."

(*Abū Dāwūd*, 4782)

Perform ablution.

The Prophet ﷺ said:

"Fire is extinguished with water, so if you become angry then perform ablution with water."

(*Abū Dāwūd*, 4784)

When you try to embody *taqwā*, you will not curse at your spouse, but you will speak kind words. You will not irrationally accuse your spouse, but you will listen wisely. You will not purposely harm your spouse, but you will respond gently.

Thus, being actively aware of Allāh Most High's presence is what will stop you from stooping to a lower level and it will motivate you to live up to your highest potential. It will keep you within a realm that protects you from evil and earns Allāh's infinite blessings.

Patience & Forgiveness

Your spouse may have annoying habits that irritate you or push your buttons from time to time. You may also be occasionally snappy and moody due to stressful situations.

Avoid finger-pointing and blaming your spouse for your reactions. No matter what your emotions tell you, you always have a choice to practice patience with your circumstances.

Own your feelings by simply admitting to yourself that you find a certain action annoying. Take a break from the situation and engage in a relaxing activity.

You can also gently let your spouse know how you feel and offer helpful suggestions of how matters can be handled differently, but it does not guarantee that things will change.

Moreover, your spouse may do things that greatly upset you. In a marriage, forgiveness is an essential ingredient for long term happiness. You cannot reach the heights of marital bliss whenever you hold on to the weight of negative feelings. It will only demotivate you from wanting to show love.

Small mistakes are easier to let go of than big hurts. This is human nature, and the reason why spouses must rely on revelation to comfort them during unexpected hurt, disappointments, and setbacks.

Allāh Most High says: "Those who spend (for Allāh's sake) in ease and in hardship, who control their anger, and who pardon others. And Allāh loves the doers of good." (*Āli ʿImrān,* 3:134)

You are not losing by being patient and forgiving. Allāh Most High loves it. If you keep this in mind, then you will soon realize that handling marital discord is not a battle between you and your spouse, but it is a test of love between you and your Creator.

> Ever since their recent trip to India, Asiya was angry at her husband Usama. In her opinion, the way he treated her and her family was unforgivable.
>
> Asiya's anger pushed her to hold back from wanting to do anything nice for Usama, and they ended up sleeping in different rooms for months.
>
> Asiya even made a list of one hundred reasons why she was angry at Usama that dated all the way back to the beginning of their marriage.
>
> One day, she came across a *ḥadīth* about forgiving others. It struck her, but she could not bring it within herself to forgive her husband.
>
> Every day she read the same *ḥadīth* and thought about the state of her marriage. Within time, she decided to forgive her husband for the sake of Allāh.

The Prophet ﷺ said, "Be merciful to others and you will be shown mercy. Forgive others and Allāh will forgive you." (*Aḥmad*, 6541)

Allāh Most High has given you the greatest motivation for why you should forgive your spouse, and it is to attain His forgiveness.

When push comes to shove, even if you do not want to forgive someone, you do it for Allāh's sake, in the hope that He will forgive you too.

The Prophet ﷺ said that no one forgives another except that Allāh increases his honor. (*Muslim*, 2588)

Pardoning another person is not a form of humiliation or degradation. By forgiving others, Allāh will raise you and honor you.

Even after you decide to forgive your spouse, you may get the urge to bring up your spouse's past wrongs. Check your intention. If you are mentioning your spouse's mistakes to sincerely help them understand something, then there is no harm.

However, if you are angrily using it to prove your point or to remind your spouse of all the good things that you have done, then it is best to avoid. You cannot move forwards if you keep traveling backwards. Forgiveness is never easy, but Allāh makes it easy through the genuineness of your faith.

Successful Muslim Couples beautify their marriage with Prophetic character. They are an example for each other in the way that they speak and act. They inspire each other towards goodness through the virtue of their own behavior.

EMOTIONAL
CONNECTION

COUPLES EXERCISE

Be open to self-improvement. Discover which things you need to change about yourself to become a better person. Use your spouse's insight as helpful clues and deepen your friendship.

Together

Choose a day and time that suits both of you. Find a relaxing place free of disruptions to attempt this exercise.

- Ask your spouse:
  - "What are three things that you like about the way that I treat you? Why does that matter to you?"
- After hearing their response, then ask:
  - "What are three things that you wish I would change about the way that I treat you? Why does that matter to you?"
- Only one person should talk, while the other person listens.

For the spouse responding to the question:

- Do answer honestly and from the heart. Help your spouse understand what you need to feel happier in the relationship.
- Do not take this as an opportunity to list all your complaints about your spouse's behavior or come down hard on them.

Focus on the top three things that they need to modify and stay positive; otherwise, you may run the risk of losing their receptiveness to change.

For the spouse listening to the answer:

- Do act interested, give your spouse time to respond, and look at your spouse while they speak.
- Do not roll your eyes, get frustrated at your spouse's delay in responding, or put down their ideas. Remain patient and give them the space to think.

Individually

After hearing what your spouse says, take some time to reflect on what was mentioned.

- Do you understand what your spouse wants from you? Why or why not?
- What steps can you take to increase the good things that you are doing and stop acting in a way that upsets your spouse?

Be a Successful Muslim Couple

Choose one of the three things that your spouse wants you to change. Strive to avoid that behavior for the next week and see if it makes a difference in your marriage.

Reflections

SECRET #5

DROP THE LABEL

There is a well-known proverb that parents sometimes teach their young children: *Sticks and stones may break my bones but names will never hurt me.*

It is often said to help children gain the confidence to overcome another person's insults. The underlying lesson is that harsh words have no impact on who you are and what you can achieve. Honestly, it is pure falsehood.

Name-calling does hurt. In fact, it stings. It makes a person doubt their capabilities, which can lead to self-esteem issues. In the long run, unchecked name-calling can become abusive and damaging to a person's soul.

The Prophet ﷺ said, "The Muslim is the one who Muslims are safe from his tongue and hands." (*Muslim*, 41)

Name-calling is more painful when it is done by someone who you admire or love, which is what makes name-calling in a marriage a deadly game to play.

Unfortunately, it is all too easy to fall into the trap of labeling your spouse with a negative name, especially when you are angry.

Sometimes you may be extremely upset and say what you feel without thinking of the consequences. Bloopers are forgivable one-offs, but unhealthy habits are recurrent patterns.

A Destructive Habit

There is an easy way to tell if you are in the habit of negatively labeling your spouse. Whenever you are irritated at what your spouse does, your sentences regularly begin with two words:

You are __________. Now fill in the blank.

Selfish. Lazy. Stupid. Inconsiderate. Uncaring. Irresponsible. Arrogant. Useless. A bad wife. A bad husband. A bad mother. A bad father. A mama's boy. A daddy's girl.

Some spouses even think that they are entitled to label their spouse, claiming that 'It is the truth. I know him / her better than anyone else!'

Others try to play it off, like what they say is just an innocent joke or a helpful comment. In return, they make their spouse wrong for getting offended at what was said.

These are all bad excuses for poor behavior. You do not have the right to insult your spouse. The only right that you have is to point out what you dislike and to ask that the action is not repeated.

If you are trying to use labeling to push your spouse to do what you want, know that it always backfires. In fact, if you regularly declare labels against your spouse, a strong resentment will grow within them towards you. No one likes to be put down, humiliated, insulted, or unappreciated.

If you continue in this direction, it may trigger your spouse to withdraw from the relationship and ignore your future requests. You can beg, plea, cry, bribe, or kick up a storm for what you want, but they remain unmoved because their heart is not with you.

On the opposite end of the spectrum, not only can labeling demotivate your spouse from wanting to please you, but it can influence you to gradually lose respect for your spouse, which in turn causes you to lose confidence in your marriage.

When you label your spouse, it blinds you from being able to see the good in the other person. Your mind quickly picks up on anything that resembles what you dislike, and that adds more fuel to the fire. You focus more on the wrong than the right, which is a recipe for marital disaster.

You do not have the right to insult your spouse. The only right that you have is to point out what you dislike and to ask that the action is not repeated.

Eventually, your vision of your spouse becomes lopsided, and you are unable to recognize your spouse for who they are as a person. In your eyes, the only thing that you know about your spouse are the labels that you have assigned to their name. Thus, labeling ultimately leads to a dead marriage.

Reasons For Labeling

Why would a spouse resort to labeling? Often enough, it happens when they are hurt by something that their spouse did or did not do. To be clear, their spouse acted in a way that the hurt spouse believes is completely unjustifiable. If the hurt spouse cannot make sense of this behavior, the labeling begins.

Initially, it is an unsaid word, like a passing thought that comes and goes. However, if the other spouse continues to repeat the same unfavorable behavior, the visiting thought turns into a plausible allegation built on top of frustration.

As time passes, the fuming frustration transforms into explosive anger that provokes harsh words to be said.

Now the tide turns. Instead of being patient with their spouse's choices, the hurt spouse automatically assumes the worst intentions. They base their opinion on the evidence that their minds have gathered to support their claims.

A label is no longer an assumption. It is a hardcore fact backed up by overwhelming proof and undeniable statistics.

The Prophetic Counsel

The Prophet ﷺ said, "A believing man should not despise a believing woman. If he finds something in her character that he dislikes, he will be pleased by something else." (*Muslim*, 1468) The same advice applies to wives.

The Prophet ﷺ teaches that no one is perfect. All humans are made of good and bad. This may be something that you can easily admit for others, but not when it comes to your spouse.

However, if you want your marriage to succeed, you need to clear your slate from a bad opinion of your partner.

The Prophet ﷺ said, "Whoever believes in Allāh and the Last Day, let him speak good or remain silent." (*Bukhārī*, 6136)

Drop the label. It only turns your spouse away from you and you away from your spouse. Don't inflict hurt on each other. Instead, consider the possibility that your spouse is a good person, but perhaps you both prioritize your responsibilities differently.

Most people do not consciously choose to upset others. Instead, they choose to act in a way that they believe is best for themselves and those around them. Your spouse probably falls into this camp of well-wishers too.

Successful Muslim Couples avoid contempt at all costs. Instead, when their spouse disappoints them, they ask their spouse why they prioritized another task over their requests.

When you try to sincerely understand the way that your spouse operates in general, and you do not take it personally, it can bring new answers to questionable behavior.

You may even increase in respect for your spouse because you admire the way that they shoulder their responsibilities. Or your spouse may be more receptive to prioritizing your needs once they see that you are sympathetic to their circumstances.

> Layla wanted her husband Uthman to fix the broken window in their house. Uthman initially agreed, but the next day, she noticed that the broken window remained untouched. She asked Uthman when he was planning on fixing it, and he replied with a vague response that he would get around to it.
>
> Layla tried to give Uthman the benefit of the doubt, but at the same time, she noticed that he was doing other things in his free time. As the days turned into nights and the weeks passed, she felt rejected. Her pain caused her to believe that her husband did not care about what she wanted.
>
> Layla started to think that her husband was inconsiderate. She often tried to meet his requests in a timely manner. Why couldn't he do the same for

her? Every time she tried to remind him; he gave a short reply that he knew. This only caused Layla's anger to grow.

Uthman was clueless about how she felt. He had no idea how much his seemingly careless decisions were pushing her over the edge.

He reasoned that the broken window is something that could be easily fixed, but he had other things on his plate that needed his attention. He did not believe that his Mr. Fix-It delay was a big deal.

One day, Layla decided to confront her husband about his unreliable behavior and how she felt about it. Puzzled by her emotions, Uthman explained that it was important for him to fix the window, but it was not pressing for him.

He reminded Layla that he does care about her, and he never thought that the delay would hurt her feelings. Shortly after, he fixed the window.

When you aim to understand your spouse's behavior instead of casting judgment on it, it connects you at a deeper level. You begin to value the fundamental features that make up your spouse's character and recognize them for the purity of their heart.

Some spouses may find that they do not respect the reasons that their spouse gives. This could occur due to conflicting personal values or deeper issues in the marriage. In these cases, it is best to seek third party support and discover solutions for how to reach common ground together.

> **When you aim to understand your spouse's behavior instead of casting judgment on it, it connects you at a deeper level. You begin to value the fundamental features that make up your spouse's character and recognize them for the purity of their heart.**

Successful Muslim Couples do not allow their personal disappointment to impact their overall view of their spouse. They are convinced that their spouse is a good person, and they avoid negatively labeling their behavior.

In its place, they seek to understand their spouse's internal decision-making process and practice patience when their views do not align.

EMOTIONAL CONNECTION

COUPLES EXERCISE

Stop labeling your spouse. Get to the crux of the matter and address what is upsetting you about their behavior. Understand each other better.

Together

Choose a day and time that suits both of you. Find a relaxing place free of disruptions to attempt this exercise.

- Mention the last time your spouse's behavior upset you by saying:

  "I felt upset when (*insert situation*). I want to hear your side. What made you believe that what you did was best?"

- Only one person should talk, while the other person listens.

- It may help to put a time limit on how long each person can speak so that one person does not dominate the conversation.

For the spouse responding to the question:

- Do answer honestly but also be sensitive to the idea that you may have hurt your spouse.

- Do not dismiss your spouse's feelings or belittle their questioning your behavior.

For the spouse listening to the answer:

- Do listen attentively and give your spouse the benefit of the doubt. Accept any apology that comes your way.
- Do not complain about the situation, accuse your spouse of ulterior motives, or declare that you do not believe them. Focus on understanding their greater intentions.

Individually

After hearing what your spouse says, take some time to reflect on what was mentioned.

- Do you sympathize with your spouse's decision? Why or why not?
- Are you able to better comprehend how they prioritize their responsibilities?
- Are you satisfied with the way that your spouse responded to your hurt feelings during the conversation?

Be a Successful Muslim Couple

Eliminate labeling from your marriage and replace it with understanding your spouse's greater intentions.

Reflections

SECRET #6

APPRECIATE STRENGTHS

The most common question that spouses ask is: "How do I get my spouse to do what I say?" The truth is that no marriage tip can guarantee that your spouse will act in the way that you want.

However, if you are hoping to learn the best tactic on how to *encourage* your spouse to do something for you, it is to compliment them. Saying kind words warms the heart, fuels the limbs, and motivates the soul to act willingly.

Perhaps you have tried this approach before. Through your gentleness, you were able to sway your work colleagues, community members, or friends.

But when was the last time you made this move on your spouse?

Once you get used to someone's presence, you tend to expect them to do what you say regardless of how you say it. You stop caring about the words used and your tone of voice.

Definitely, the more you become comfortable with your spouse, the more you become comfortable with making demands and declaring ultimatums.

However, your spouse is not your employee, your servant, or your robot. They are your partner, your friend, and your equal. The way that you ask for things matters, and your appreciation for their contributions weighs heavily on their heart.

The Prophet ﷺ said, "Whoever does not thank the people does not thank Allāh." (*Tirmidhī*, 1954)

Every time you overlook appreciating your spouse, you overlook an opportunity to thank Allāh for a blessing that He gave you. Your spouse's actions are willed by Allāh Most

High, and He is the source of any good that comes to you. Therefore, anytime your spouse does something nice for you, it should not be taken for granted, no matter how small the act.

Allāh Most High says: "…If you are grateful, I will certainly give you more." (*Ibrāhīm*, 14:7)

By appreciating your spouse, you gain Allāh's blessings in this life and a mighty reward in the Hereafter. Thus, showing appreciation for your spouse's good deeds must be intentional and consistent.

What To Appreciate

It is a common misconception that appreciation is the equivalent of saying thank you, but appreciation in a marriage is much more.

Appreciation means to identify the qualities that make your spouse special to you. It is the act of noticing and acknowledging what makes you grateful for having your spouse in your life, and then letting your spouse know how you feel about it.

Qualities to appreciate are:

- Being a great listener and friend.
- Being helpful and dependable during hard times.
- Being supportive with your goals and ambitions.
- Being positive and upbeat when you are feeling low.
- Being loyal and trustworthy when you are uncertain.

- Being understanding and accommodating when you make mistakes.
- Being able to make you laugh and smile when you are upset.
- Being generous with money and time.
- Being respectful towards your family and friends.
- Being dedicated to parenting your children and nursing elderly parents.

Because you each bring different strengths to the relationship, you may be grateful for different things. Often enough, your weaknesses are your spouse's strengths, and your strengths are your spouse's weaknesses.

You both balance each other out with the unique qualities that you bring to the relationship. So, the point is not to give the same compliments but to give credit where credit is due.

> Malika and Sajid have been married for over forty-five years. They both have contrasting personalities, which surprisingly only added a richness to their relationship.
>
> Malika was strong willed, determined, and forward thinking. She was good with money and had a strong passion for running businesses. Sajid was laid back, gentle, and sweet. He was great with people and had a love for family ties.
>
> When asked what makes their marriage special, they both expressed their gratitude for the other person's

qualities. It was a team effort that made their marriage good.

Sajid liked how much Malika was able to accomplish tasks, manage responsibilities, and keep things moving ahead. She regularly scheduled his doctors' appointments and kept their home organized.

Malika admired her husband's considerate nature, thoughtfulness, and companionship. He bought the groceries, regularly complimented her cooking, and made her laugh all the time.

They were grateful to have each other in their lives and tried to not lose touch of the blessing of their friendship by thanking each other as much as possible.

The Unexpressive Spouse

Sometimes spouses purposely withhold appreciation from each other. They think that saying something nice will make the other person conceited or influence them to stop working hard. Some may assert that their spouse already knows how they feel and there is no point in stating the obvious. Yet, nothing could be further from the truth.

When you deny appreciating your spouse, they lose the enthusiasm to please you. This can cause the relationship to deteriorate. Conversely, when you actively recognize the good qualities of your spouse and compliment their capabilities, it makes them feel valued, confident, and willing to give back more.

Furthermore, appreciation results in your happiness. When you appreciate someone, you treat them differently. Without that feeling, you can behave cold, mean, indifferent, or antagonistic. By appreciating your spouse, you remember why you love them. This causes you to enjoy their company and serve them happily.

Thus, expressing appreciation is a vital aspect of marital satisfaction, and it is a win-win situation for everyone.

Some spouses may find it hard and against their nature to express themselves. Perhaps they express their love through their actions more than their words.

However, creating a successful marriage requires that you step out of your comfort zone and do what it takes to solidify your friendship as a couple.

- ☑ Start off by scheduling in at least one verbal appreciation a day.
- ☑ As for the spouse who feels unappreciated, you must gently remind your spouse that you need words of affirmation – without accusing them of being a bad spouse or implying it.
- ☑ Instigate a response by leading by example. Show your own appreciation and ask your spouse to join in by adding their thoughts about you.

It may not be what you want, but alternative solutions are needed when dealing with spouses who are unfamiliar with how to express themselves.

Nitpickers & Micromanagers

A nitpicker is someone who finds faults, no matter how small or unimportant. A micromanager is someone who attempts to control how their spouse spends their time and energy. People with these personality traits are often high achievers, detailed-oriented, or perfectionists.

There are a couple of reasons why a person falls into a pattern of nitpicking or micromanaging. Some saw their parents act in this manner, and they obliviously mimic their behavior. Because it was considered 'normal' in their household, they do not realize the negative impact that their behavior has on their spouse.

Others are provoked by fear and worry. They are convinced that something bad will happen if they do not step in and offer their input. It is difficult for them to relinquish control and trust that their spouse is fully competent and capable without them.

Regardless of the reason, the spouse on the receiving end usually feels belittled, inadequate, criticized, and suffocated. Consequently, this is a cause of frequent conflict between the two, especially when the nitpicker / micromanager shoots down their spouse's frequent complaints about their behavior.

The Prophet ﷺ said, "Make things easy for people and do not make things difficult for them." (*Bukhārī*, 6125)

If your behavior is pushing another person to feel constrained and overwhelmed, you need to change it for the sake of Allāh. Become more balanced in the way you act and speak.

☑ Draw a line between problems that demand your attention and issues that can be overlooked. Learn to pick your battles and save your feedback for the big issues.

The Prophet ﷺ said, "Verily, Allāh is gentle, and He loves gentleness. He rewards for gentleness what is not granted for harshness, and He does not reward anything else like it." (*Muslim*, 4593)

Be more thoughtful in how you explain your views. It may help to sandwich negative statements between positive statements. This way your spouse will not interpret your comments as harsh criticism.

On another note, sometimes spouses declare that their spouse does not have any praiseworthy characteristics. Don't be so quick to judge. Question the validity of these thoughts.

Could it be that you are overlooking your spouse's good qualities because you are comparing them to others? Are you resentful about something else? Get clear on the real reason.

Allāh Most High says, "And live with them in kindness. For if you dislike them, then perhaps you dislike a thing and Allāh makes much good therein." (*al-Nisā'*, 4:19)

No one is perfect except Allāh. Through His infinite knowledge and power, He gifted you with your spouse, and He knows what is best for you. So, if your spouse brings any goodness into your life, direct your gaze towards that blessing and steer clear of black-and-white thinking.

The Prophet ﷺ said, "A kind word is charity." (*Bukhārī*, 2989)

Don't hold back. Give as much charity as you can in your marriage. Allāh will reward you for every word you donate.

Successful Muslim Couples admire each other's strengths and good qualities. They regularly voice their satisfaction with each other. They grow in love by showing their appreciation.

EMOTIONAL CONNECTION

COUPLES EXERCISE

Appreciate your spouse frequently. Find reasons to compliment them, acknowledge their good deeds, and express gratitude for their excellent qualities. Improve your friendship and solidify your love.

Together

Choose a day and time that suits both of you. Find a relaxing place free of disruptions to attempt this exercise.

- Take turns expressing what you appreciate about the other person. Mention at least three things.
- Use simple phrases like:
  - "I love that you…"
  - "I want you to know that I am really grateful for…"
  - "I can never thank you enough for…"
- Only one person should talk, while the other person listens.
- Do not put a time limit on the conversation. Enjoy the positive vibe and go with the flow.

For the spouse showing appreciation:

- Do speak honestly and from the heart. Let your spouse know how much they mean to you.

- Do not mix compliments and criticism together. Keep the conversation positive.

For the spouse listening to the appreciation:

- Do smile and act happy with what your spouse says.
- Do not put down your spouse's ideas. Accept any compliments that come your way.

Individually

After hearing what your spouse says, take some time to reflect on what was mentioned.

- Do you feel appreciated in your marriage? Why or why not?
- How often should your spouse do this exercise with you?
- What steps can you take to show more appreciation for your spouse's contributions?

Be a Successful Muslim Couple

Every day for the next week tell your spouse why you appreciate them. Intend to make it a consistent habit.

Reflections

PART 3

PHYSICAL CONNECTION

A physical connection keeps you sexually attracted to each other and makes you lifetime lovers. It is to honor each other's needs for affection inside and outside the bedroom.

PHYSICAL
CONNECTION

COUPLES QUIZ

Take this quiz to discover the strength of your physical connection. For every statement that you agree with, give yourselves a point. Read about your score afterwards and the marriage tips that follow.

- ☐ We feel sexually attracted to each other.
- ☐ We regularly call each other by endearing nicknames.
- ☐ We try to look good and smell nice for each other.
- ☐ We verbally compliment each other's physical features.
- ☐ We regularly exchange non-sexual touches in the form of hugs, innocent kisses, and holding hands.
- ☐ We are both satisfied with our overall sex life as a couple.
- ☐ We both make time to engage in marital relations.
- ☐ We try to fulfill each other's sexual desires and fantasies.
- ☐ We can openly talk about which actions we like and dislike in the bedroom.
- ☐ We do not make the other person feel bad for not wanting to do what the other person prefers in the bedroom.

Scores

9 to 10

Māshā'Allāh you are both attentive to each other's physical needs and have a strong intimate connection. May Allāh continue to bless it.

6 to 8

You may both feel attracted to each other but perhaps you need a better understanding of how to fulfill each other's sexual needs. Try to create more passion with the tips that follow *insha'Allāh*.

Below 5

You both may not see eye-to-eye on bedroom matters. This can happen in marriages. Make improving your physical connection a priority. See if the upcoming advice helps you to get connected *insha'Allāh*.

Reflections

SECRET #7

EMBRACE HIM & HER

Adam was introduced to Aisha by a work colleague who thought that they would make a good match. They were both religious, Syrian, in their early twenties, and family oriented.

They were settled in different countries and had to perform their marriage contract (*nikāh*) via the internet. The relationship would briefly continue as long distance until they could organize their living arrangements to be together.

After they became *ḥalāl* for each other, Aisha became a different woman. When they had video calls, Aisha would style her hair, wear makeup, and dress in tight clothing. She giggled at Adam's jokes and was very fun to be around. They both spoke for hours every day.

Adam lost over ten kilos purely from being enamored by her presence. He could not eat or drink. He only longed to be around her and give her everything she wanted.

It is no secret that men are instinctively attracted to women and women are instinctively attracted to men.

The million-dollar question is: How do you make that attraction last in a marriage?

When the excitement of finding your beloved quiets down, so can the initial high of being sexually attracted to each other. Lovemaking becomes routine. Touching can feel less affectionate. In truth, keeping interest in your spouse takes concentrated effort.

Allāh Most High says: "And the male is not like the female." (*Āli 'Imrān*, 3:36)

Allāh Most High created men and women to be different for a reason, and appreciating these differences are for your benefit.

Different does not mean that one gender is bad and the other is better. Rather, when these differences are validated and accepted, they flatter each other, especially in a romantic relationship.

Men are naturally drawn to a woman's feminine flare, and women are naturally drawn to a man's masculine charm. This polarity in genders is what pulls each person to the other, thus creating a magnetic attraction and a strong sexual dynamic.

Successful Muslim Couples embrace their God-given gender roles and use their innate talents to keep the passion alive in their marriage.

Different does not mean that one gender is bad and the other is better. Rather, when these differences are validated and accepted, they flatter each other, especially in a romantic relationship.

Embrace Him

A woman's attraction to her husband is based heavily on her emotions and how she feels about him. If you want to keep your wife interested in you, then consider these tips.

Women are attracted to a man who can:

Take initiative: When a man is successful at what he does and is determined to achieve, a woman cannot help but notice. She admires his leadership traits and feels proud of her husband.

Therefore, when brothers spend endless hours playing video games or watching movies on their phones, it is a huge turn off. Needing downtime is acceptable, but squandering your free time is irresponsible.

Making excuses for it will only trigger your wife's motherly instincts, and she will treat you like a child.

Provide: When a man takes responsibility to financially provide for his wife and family, it increases a woman's appreciation for him in her life. She will naturally want to reward the favor by being a pleasant partner.

However, paying bills is not the only thing that she wants. A woman hopes that her husband will buy her thoughtful gifts and be willing to spend on her beyond his obligatory duties.

The Prophet ﷺ said, "Give gifts and you will love one another." (*al-Adab al-Mufrad*, 594)

Gifts do not need to be expensive, just thoughtful. When a husband is uncaring and cheap, a wife quickly loses interest.

Show generosity: Being generous is not just about money. It also includes being giving with your free time and being considerate in your character.

When a man is willing to spend regular time with his wife and listen to her speak about her life, it is extremely attractive. It sends the message that he cares about her.

You only need to focus on listening to her. Unless your wife asks, you do not need to provide a solution for everything that she speaks about, which can feel very unnatural for some men.

Moreover, when you show consideration for the effort that she puts into the family, she feels cherished and adored.

Conversely, when brothers spend all their free time with their friends, parents, or other family members, a wife will feel ignored. Even worse, when he overlooks her contributions, she will feel rejected. All of this can cause her to question the quality of the relationship and be less willing to be your lover.

Speak sweet words: Whether it was through fairytale books or movies, most women grew up hearing about the concept of Romeo and Juliet.

As such, women expect that men will automatically be programmed to say loving words, call them by endearing names, and compliment their beauty.

Most men are not hardwired to initiate sweet words. However, if you want your wife to stay attracted to you, you must learn how to be her version of Romeo.

The Prophet ﷺ would call the Mother of the Believers ʿĀʾisha ؓ '*Humayra*' (Little Rosey One) as a compliment for her beautiful, reddish complexion. (*Ibn Mājah*, 2474) He would also shorten her name and affectionately call her '*Āʾish.*' (*Bukhārī*, 3768)

When you habitually call your wife cute names, it warms her heart, and when you consistently tell your wife that she is beautiful and sexy, it increases her confidence in herself and her body.

Furthermore, be kind in the way you respond to her emotions. Comfort and console her. Avoid yelling at her and making her feel bad. When the Prophet ﷺ found Lady ʿĀʾisha رضي الله عنها crying because she started menstruating during *ḥajj*, he ﷺ eased her worries with words that warmed her heart. (*Bukhārī*, 305)

Look presentable: When a man looks suave, chic, and sophisticated, it draws attention from all corners of the room. For this reason, brothers often think that they need to workout at the gym and buy designer clothes to look nice.

Every woman will differ on what she wants, but most of the time, it is not about having big muscles or expensive clothes. It is more about looking neat.

Brothers need to take care of themselves too. Make sure you maintain a decent weight, smell nice, trim your beard, and dress in clean clothes.

The Prophet ﷺ said:

> **"Four things are from the Sunna of the messengers: modesty, applying attar, using the tooth stick (*siwāk*), and marriage."**

(*Tirmidhī*, 1080)

Lena and Munir both worked from home. They had different jobs, but working remotely meant that they would see each other all the time. They grew used to each other's company, and their relationship developed into a cozy friendship.

Even though they were emotionally close, Lena felt like something was missing from their marriage. They frequently stayed at home and worked nonstop hours.

Lena suggested that they break out of their normal routine and go on a date together. Munir agreed and thought carefully about where to go.

He decided to take Lena downtown. They casually walked around and window shopped. Munir then treated her to a meal. Both spent the night catching up on each other's thoughts about life. As Lena looked at her husband speak, she became more attracted to him.

It wasn't only because of what he was saying, but it was everything all together. She admired his kindness and giving nature. She felt taken care of and special.

When they returned home, Lena gave Munir a warm hug and a kiss. She expressed how much they needed to commit to regular dates so that they stayed connected like a normal couple.

Embrace Her

Telling a woman to be feminine can create mixed feelings amongst sisters. Part of the hesitation returns to not wanting to be controlled, dumbed down, or used as a doormat.

Getting in touch with who you are as a woman will do nothing of the sort. It is more about becoming clued up on how to keep the passion alive in your marriage.

Men are attracted to a woman who can:

Look good: Men want their wives to look pretty inside their homes. This can be achieved, for example, by wearing colorful clothing, doing your hair, and wearing perfume.

Sometimes sisters care more about what they look like when they leave their homes than what they wear behind closed doors.

It is normal to want to feel comfortable in your house, but habitually wearing old t-shirts and bedroom slippers can greatly disappoint your husband.

Ask your husband what he likes to see you in. When you care about what you look like, he will feel excited to be with you.

Be confident in their sexuality: In today's times, it is difficult to feel confident about your own body. You could be blessed with a great figure, but when you compare yourself to other women on social media, they may look prettier.

This then puts a damper on your self-esteem, which can make sexiness appear like an unachievable goal.

The truth is that you do not need to impress the entire world, just your husband. He didn't marry you because he thought you were ugly and needed improvement. He chose you because he saw someone that he wanted to be with for a lifetime.

For many Muslim husbands, they want their wives to 'act' sexy. That translates into flirting with him. Being playful, giggling, smiling, and flipping your hair are all examples of flirtatious behavior. Tap into your feminine energy and get confident in your own skin.

Take care of him: Every husband wants a woman who he can count on for comfort and care. When a man feels like he is low priority for his wife, he will be less attracted to her.

The Prophet ﷺ said:

> **"Any woman who dies whilst her husband is pleased with her will enter Paradise."**

(*Tirmidhī*, 1161)

Pleasing your husband is a gate to eternal bliss. Every man will differ on what this means. Refer to Secret #2 for ideas of how to know your husband's core needs for love.

Be friendly: In the heart of every man is a desire for a companion. Being a friend means that you are respectful and encouraging of his pursuits. When women speak harshly and are argumentative, it hurts their husbands.

This does not mean that you cannot speak up for your needs or mark boundaries. Rather, it is all about the way you do it. You can get what you want if your approach is inviting.

The Prophet ﷺ advised, "Marry the fertile and loving woman." (*Abū Dāwūd*, 2050; *Nasā'ī*, 3227)

Men are drawn to a woman's tenderness and softness. They want to rescue their wives, protect them, and provide for them. By being a loving friend, you compel him to take care of you and it keeps him wanting to be with you.

You can read about more wife tips in the book "Say It With Love: Communicate, Connect & Cure Conflict" by Naielah Ackbarali.

Be happy: Men are attracted to women who are upbeat and positive. Your husband wants to see you smile. He takes pride in your happiness and feels at ease with your joy.

Frequently frowning, crying, being pessimistic, and showing ingratitude will only chase him away.

The Prophet ﷺ said, "Allāh does not look (with mercy) at a woman who is ungrateful to her husband whilst she is dependent on him (for her livelihood)." (*Nasā'ī*, 9086)

Rejoice in the blessings that Allāh Most High grants you through your husband.

Successful Muslim Couples continue to be sexually attracted to each other throughout their marriage. They make the moves to stay interested in one another by the way they act, speak, and dress.

PHYSICAL CONNECTION

COUPLES EXERCISE

Appreciate your spouse's masculine and feminine energy. Compliment their appearance, manly strengths, and feminine gifts. Keep your love alive with words of admiration.

Together

Choose a day and time that suits both of you. Find a relaxing place free of disruptions to attempt this exercise.

- Take turns expressing what you find attractive about the other person. Mention at least three things.
- Use simple phrases like:
  - "I love your…"
  - "I am really attracted to you because…"
  - "I get excited thinking about…"
- Only one person should talk, while the other person listens.
- Do not put a time limit on the conversation. Enjoy the positive vibe and go with the flow.

For the spouse complimenting:

- Do answer honestly and from the heart. Let your spouse know what you like about them.

- Do not insult your spouse's physical appearance or suggest improvements at this point.

For the spouse receiving the compliment:

- Do smile and act happy with what your spouse says, even if you find some comments surprising.
- Do not roll your eyes or reject their ideas. Accept any compliment that comes your way.

Individually

After hearing what your spouse says, take some time to reflect on what was mentioned.

- Do you feel attractive in your marriage? Why or why not?
- How often should your spouse do this exercise with you?
- What steps can you take to be more sexually attractive to your spouse?

Be a Successful Muslim Couple

Care about your sex appeal and do what it takes to remain attractive to your spouse.

Reflections

SECRET #8

GIVE SADAQA

The Prophet ﷺ said, "…and in a man engaging in sexual intercourse with his wife, there is a charity (*ṣadaqa*)."

The Companions ﷺ said, "O Messenger of Allāh, one of us fulfills his sexual desires and he is given a reward for it?"

He ﷺ responded, "Do you not see that if he were to fulfill it through something forbidden it would be a sin against him? Similarly, if he were to fulfill it through something lawful, he will be rewarded."

(*Muslim*, 1006)

From His immense generosity, Allāh Most High made marital relations an act that reaps reward in the Hereafter. Marital intercourse becomes an act of worship through a person's intention. For example, making the intention to fulfill the rights of one's spouse, to treat them kindly, to give birth to a righteous child, or to keep oneself or one's spouse chaste.

With the rise of the porn industry and the spread of indecency, the idea of what sex is has become warped. Sex has transformed into a selfish individualistic deed based on distorted fantasies, rather than fulfilling normal physical needs between two people who love each other.

In Islam, sexual intercourse is not only about pleasing yourself, but it is about staying in a realm that pleases Allāh Most High. For this reason, the topic of sexual intercourse between spouses must be approached from a spiritual perspective; otherwise, sex becomes one-sided, animalistic, or unfulfilling.

Marital relations should be based on the Prophet's words of giving charity (*ṣadaqa*). When spouses bear in mind that they must give to the other person, instead of only thinking of themselves, bedroom matters become more enjoyable.

Successful Muslim Couples tend to their physical connection and make it a priority. They give habitual *ṣadaqa* to their spouses inside the bedroom, as well as outside.

Sadaqa Outside the Bedroom

Giving *ṣadaqa* outside the bedroom builds greater chemistry between spouses inside the bedroom. Creating intimacy outside the bedroom consists of keeping your heart connection and emotional connection strong, as well as being physically affectionate with each other.

Both men and women need physical affection. Touch says what words cannot. Through a warm touch, you reaffirm your bond as a couple.

Holding hands, cuddling, kissing, hugging, squeezing, caressing, and giving massages are all ways to strengthen the ties of your relationship.

With each gesture, it is as if you are sending sweet love messages to your spouse, like "I love you. I care about you. I notice you. I want to be with you."

This is why physical affection can help build more trust between spouses and amplify overall satisfaction within the relationship. Small acts of affection also keep romance at the forefront of the marriage.

The Prophet ﷺ kissed his wives even when he was fasting. (*Bukhārī*, 1928)

He ﷺ lovingly drank from the same spot of the cup of Lady ʿĀʾisha ؓ. (*Muslim*, 300)

He would lay next to Umm Salama رضي الله عنها under the same cover even though she was menstruating. (*Bukhārī*, 322)

Lady ʿĀʾisha رضي الله عنها would comb his hair and he ﷺ would lie in her lap while reciting Qur'ān. (*Bukhārī*, 295; 297)

Successful Muslim Couples touch their spouses on multiple occasions throughout the day. Whether it be a kiss before leaving for work in the morning, holding hands when walking, massages at the end of the day, or a tender cuddle before sleeping at nighttime, they stay physically connected. This results in better bedroom relations.

Physical connection weakens when spouses argue and do not make up. When you are angry at your spouse, you feel emotionally distant from them and you may be tempted to avoid touching them.

Once couples hold back from touching outside the bedroom, they often stop touching inside the bedroom, and their sex life ultimately suffers.

As unnatural as it may seem, these are the moments when you need to go beyond your upset feelings and freely show affection. Touching during conflict helps melt away the bad feelings and it restores your severed connection. A soft touch on the hand, an arm around the shoulder, or a gentle embrace can overpower negative emotion.

Being physically affectionate is often instinctive to those who grew up in families that showed affection. Even if you are not naturally inclined towards showing affection, do not assume that your spouse is satisfied with your inaction. They may need your tender touch more than you may think.

If your spouse is not accustomed to initiating physical affection, practice patience when they forget or overlook being affectionate.

Try to teach your spouse to be more affectionate by stating your needs and leading by example. A person who feels loved, cared for, and adored is more likely to reciprocate in kind.

Avoid holding back the love just because you are hurt. Think of the bigger picture of keeping your marriage blissful and peaceful. Every spouse makes mistakes from time to time.

Another issue is that sometimes spouses avoid showing affection outside of the bedroom because they are afraid that it will lead to sexual intercourse. They are happy to kiss and touch, but they do not want it to go further.

This is a topic that each couple must discuss with each other and decide what is best for their relationship. You could agree that any touch during the day is for play, whereas touch at nighttime can progress into something more substantial.

Do not cut out affection altogether. When you continue to be intimate with each other outside the bedroom, you continue to keep the doors open for intimacy inside the bedroom.

Sadaqa Inside the Bedroom

Successful Muslim Couples enjoy pleasing their spouses for the sake of Allāh Most High. They go beyond viewing marital relations as merely a 'duty' or a 'right.'

Instead, they engage in marital intercourse out of love and care for the other person. This beautifies their lovemaking. Transform your approach to marital relations with a more compassionate perspective.

1. Be Sensual: Avoid rushing to reach the end. Take your time and build up to engaging in marital relations. Explore each other's bodies and experiment with what is pleasurable.

Make sure that your spouse is on the same page as you move along. Simply asking if they are enjoying the moment can help improve further communication around sexual issues. Inquire about what they prefer and what makes them happy. Sometimes they may be unsure, but that's all the reason to keep exploring together.

Moreover, take any necessary steps beforehand to get yourself in the mood and be ready for the act. For example, some sisters enjoy marital relations more when they take a moment to clear their minds of their to-do-lists, dress up in lingerie, and wind down into a relaxing state.

Let your spouse know if there is anything that they can do to help you be more present for the occasion as well.

2. Make A Date: After having children, it may become more difficult to schedule in spontaneous bedroom time. Couples with children should agree on days and times for lovemaking. You must give priority to your physical connection, even if you are busy or tired.

Some spouses overlook this important factor in their relationship. Unfortunately, the other spouse often ends up becoming sexually frustrated and dissatisfied with their spouse's lack of attention. They may feel like their physical needs are neglected and ignored, which can cause huge resentment to form.

The Prophet ﷺ regularly made love to his wives رضي الله عنهن despite all his duties. He ﷺ also remained intimate with his wives during their menstruation by touching them above their lower garment, despite sexual intercourse being prohibited. (*Abū Dāwūd*, 2167)

By agreeing on days and times, you can better schedule what to do on that day so that you are not tired or busied away from the bedroom at night. It may help to remind each other in the morning that today is a 'lovemaking day.' This way you are each attentive to what the evening will bring.

> Rahima and Yusuf had been married for over ten years. After their most recent child was born it was difficult to even think of having marital relations again. They were both too busy with the new baby and their other children's needs.
>
> Not wanting their love life to suffer, they decided to agree on days and times to make love. Rahima would take it easy on those days and not cook big meals or deep clean the house. She would try to save her energy for nighttime. Yusuf would offer to buy takeout and do whatever he could to remove the extra load off her shoulders.

3. Agree On Fantasies: After many years of marriage, a common issue that arises amongst couples is avoiding boredom in the bedroom. Marital relations can seem like a routine chore if you do not actively make it different.

Avoid engaging in intercourse the same way all the time. Break out of your comfort zone and be open to trying something new. The variation in styles builds enthusiasm and a better physical connection.

You each may have different sexual desires and fantasies. It is important that you both agree on which actions can be taken to please each other. If you overlook this step, you may risk turning your spouse away, which defeats the purpose.

Stick to what you both feel comfortable doing. If you are hoping for something more, share your ideas with your spouse, without making them feel bad if they do not conform to what you want. Marital relations should be mutually satisfying and fulfilling, not one-sided.

Moreover, you may want marital relations more frequently than your spouse, or vice versa. It is quite common for spouses to have mismatched sex drives. Sometimes it is from external factors. For example, for many women their drives can differ due to hormonal fluctuations from aging or after giving birth.

You must cooperate with each other and be understanding of each other's circumstances. Do not blame your spouse for wanting too much or being satisfied with too little. Ignoring the fact that your spouse may feel rejected or exhausted will only negatively impact your connection.

No one's sex drive is permanently fixed. Adapt to each other's needs as they change throughout your relationship. Try to reach a common ground on what you both feel is necessary at this point in your life and strive to live up to that standard.

The spirit of marital relations must revolve around the spirit of giving *ṣadaqa*. Being charitable is a willingness to be fully selfless, even if you may be the neediest.

Successful Muslim Couples are keen to fulfill each other's sexual needs and desires. They stay physically connected with warm touches inside and outside the bedroom.

PHYSICAL CONNECTION

COUPLES EXERCISE

Get physically connected inside and outside the bedroom. Discover what your spouse needs to feel sexually satisfied.

Together

Choose a day and time that suits both of you. Find a relaxing place free of disruptions to attempt this exercise.

- Ask your spouse:
  - "Are you satisfied with how frequently we touch outside the bedroom? Which types of touch do you like the most?"
  - "Are you satisfied with how frequently we touch inside the bedroom? Which types of touch do you like the most?"
  - "Does anything need to change for our sex life to get better?"
- Only one person should talk, while the other person listens.

For the spouse responding to the question:

- Do answer honestly and from the heart. Let your spouse know what you would like.
- Do not insult your spouse's lovemaking skills or inability to show affection.

For the spouse listening to the answer:

- Do listen attentively and be open to learning about what would help better your physical connection.
- Do not roll your eyes, get frustrated at your spouse's delay in responding, or reject their ideas.

Individually

After hearing what your spouse says, take some time to reflect on what was mentioned.

- Did you feel comfortable having this conversation with your spouse? Why or why not?
- Were you both able to agree on which steps to take to become a more sexually satisfied couple?
- Are you willing to give more touch outside or inside the bedroom? Why or why not?

Be a Successful Muslim Couple

Strive to be more affectionate outside the bedroom this week and note if it improves your connection as a couple.

Reflections

PART 4

SPIRITUAL CONNECTION

A spiritual connection is the ultimate connection. It is to help each other excel spiritually for the sake of Allāh Most High and to be partners in faith through the thick and thin.

SPIRITUAL
CONNECTION

COUPLES QUIZ

Take this quiz to discover the strength of your spiritual connection. For every statement that you agree with, give yourselves a point. Read about your score afterwards and the marriage tips that follow.

- ☐ We pray and fast together.
- ☐ We structure our lives around Islamic teachings.
- ☐ We agree on how to spend time as a couple during Fridays, Ramadan, and Eid holidays.
- ☐ We do not have major disagreements over religious matters.
- ☐ We remind each other about what Islam says with regards to doing good deeds and avoiding sins.
- ☐ We agree on how to raise our children religiously.
- ☐ We both feel like the other person has our back, no matter what.
- ☐ We both believe that our relationship gets deeper and more meaningful over time.
- ☐ We know what the other needs under stress.
- ☐ We have gone through difficulties together and have become stronger in faith and in love through them.

Scores

9 to 10

Māshā'Allāh you are both striving to please Allāh Most High in your marriage. May Allāh continue to bless your intentions and give you success (*tawfīq*) in achieving them.

6 to 8

You are both concerned about your faith, but you may not be working together as a team. Try to establish better habits as a couple with the tips that follow *insha'Allāh*.

Below 5

Your spiritual connection is not as strong as it could be. Perhaps you both have different ideas and goals around your spirituality. See if the upcoming advice helps you to reach a similar understanding *insha'Allāh*.

Reflections

SECRET #9

FORM GOOD HABITS

The Prophet ﷺ said that a person will taste the sweetness of faith when he loves someone purely for the sake of Allāh. (*Bukhārī*, 16)

Loving someone for Allāh's sake means that your love is not based upon worldly gain, but it is rooted in how much the other person reminds you of Allāh Most High.

Most certainly, when you love a person for Allāh, He places countless blessings in your relationship and it will be the best love that you experience.

Successful Muslim Couples love each other for the sake of Allāh Most High. They admire and appreciate each other's spiritual strengths. They sacrifice their worldly desires to keep the peace between their hearts. They find the sweetness of faith in the sincerity of their interactions, companionship, and friendship.

The Prophet ﷺ said that one of the best types of wealth is a believing wife who can help a man on his faith. (*Tirmidhī*, 3094)

Successful Muslim Couples remind each other to be better believers.

They encourage each other to do good deeds.

They guard each other from committing sins.

They know the worth of being spiritual partners, and they treasure the value of worshipping Allāh together.

Every couple should aim to fill their household with blessings (*baraka*). By establishing good spiritual habits with each other, you are more likely to reap the reward of a peaceful, serene home.

1. Give salām together.

The Prophet ﷺ said, "You will not enter Paradise until you have faith and you will not have faith until you love each other. Shall I show you something that if you did it, you would love each other? Spread the (greeting of) *salām* between yourselves." (*Muslim*, 54)

Every time you enter your household, give the *salām* to your spouse. Whenever you have been apart for some time, greet your spouse warmly and ask how they are. Show your spouse that you care about their presence. It will increase your blessings and your love for each other.

Praying together will keep you both focused on what truly matters in life, which is to please Allāh Most High. It will protect you from treating each other offensively.

2. Pray together.

Allāh Most High says: "…And establish prayer. Indeed, prayer prohibits immorality and wrongdoing, and the remembrance of Allāh is greater." (*al- 'Ankabūt*, 29:45)

Praying together will keep you both focused on what truly matters in life, which is to please Allāh Most High. It will protect you from treating each other offensively and committing actions that earn Allāh's wrath.

Prayer will motivate you to be good to each other, even during times when you are angry or hurt. The Prophet ﷺ prayed with his wives رضي الله عنهن too. Couples who pray together stay together.

3. Fast together.

The Prophet ﷺ said there is a gate in Paradise called *ar-Rayyān*, and only those who fast will enter it and no one else will enter it. (*Bukhārī*, 1896)

- Enter Paradise through the same gate. Fast *Ramaḍān* together and whatever you can manage from voluntary fasts.
- Create a family tradition of breaking fast at the same time and eating *ifṭār* with each other.
- Gather your children together and make a group *du'ā'*.

Samira and Khalid had been married for two years. They were both converts to Islam and lived away from their extended families.

Samira was invited to a ladies' only *ifṭār*. She initially accepted because she wanted to have fun with her friends. Khalid stayed at home and broke his fast by himself, while Samira talked and laughed with her friends. As Samira sat down to eat her plate of food, she felt troubled.

Was her husband eating all by himself in *Ramaḍān* while she was having fun? It hurt her to think of her husband being alone without any company.

She immediately jumped up, excused herself, and ran home to eat *ifṭār* with her husband. Thereafter, they established a strong family tradition of being together for *ifṭār*, unless they were both invited out.

4. Eat together.

The Prophet ﷺ said, "Eat your meals together and mention the name of Allāh over it, for you will be blessed in it." (*Abū Dāwūd*, 3764) Food unites hearts.

- Try to eat at least one meal together daily.
- Use this time to catch up on each other's lives, laugh, and be friends.
- Keep up with this habit after having children so that you give them good memories of their childhood.

5. Make duʿāʾ together.

The Prophet ﷺ said, "If you ask, then ask Allāh, and if you seek help, then seek help from Allāh." (*Tirmidhī*, 2516)

Tap into the power of *duʿāʾ* and ask Allāh to remove the difficulties and trials that you face as a couple.

- Make *duʿāʾ* for your spouse when they are sick.
- Make *duʿāʾ* for righteous children and a blissful marriage.
- Make *duʿāʾ* for lawful provision.

Let *duʿāʾ* be what gives you hope.

Recommended Duas

رَبَّنَا هَبْ لَنَا مِنْ أَزْوَاجِنَا وَذُرِّيَّاتِنَا قُرَّةَ أَعْيُنٍ

وَاجْعَلْنَا لِلْمُتَّقِينَ إِمَامًا

Rabbanā hab lanā min azwājinā wa dhurriyyātinā qurrata ʾaʿyun wajʿalnā lil muttaqīna imāmā

"Our Lord! Bless us with pious spouses and offspring who will be the joy of our hearts and make us models for the righteous."

(*al-Furqān*, 25:74)

رَبَّنَا آتِنَا فِي الدُّنْيَا حَسَنَةً وَفِي الآخِرَةِ حَسَنَةً

وقِنَا عَذَابَ النَّارِ

Rabbanā ātinā fid dunyā ḥasanatan wa fil ākhirati ḥasanatan waqinā ʿadhāb an-nār

"Our Lord, grant us what is good of this world and the Hereafter, and protect us from the punishment of the Fire."

(*al-Baqara*, 2:201)

6. Be charitable together.

The Prophet ﷺ said, "Charity extinguishes sins just as water extinguishes fire." (*Tirmidhī*, 614)

- Clear your slates by donating money to a charitable cause together.
- Take care of elderly parents together.
- Volunteer your time to help with community projects together.

Be mindful of others and Allāh will be mindful of you.

> Muhsin and Zaynab were married for almost twenty years. They had several children and desired for all of them to memorize the Qur'ān. They traveled to different countries to provide their children with the best Islamic education.
>
> Even though they were busy with raising their children, they gave back to the greater community by hosting and organizing events with scholars.
>
> Zaynab helped pull things together on the ladies' side, while Muhsin took charge of the men's arrangements. They connected as a couple through their common interest of wanting to serve others and admired these qualities in each other.

7. Raise your kids together.

The Prophet ﷺ said, "When a person dies, all his deeds come to an end except three: continuous charity, knowledge that benefits, and a righteous child that prays for him." (*Muslim*, 1631)

Islam is a communal religion, and the community starts at home. Give your children the best medicine for a sound emotional state and confidence in their religion: a happy home. Through your marriage, you call them to the beautiful teachings of Islam.

Be a parenting team.

- Help each other and be considerate of each other's efforts.
- Do not fight in front of your children and do not neglect their need to see that you are in a good marriage.
- Be a positive influence on their hearts and religious outlook.
- Keep the child's best interests in mind, and not just what you want.

Give your children the best medicine for a sound emotional state and confidence in their religion: a happy home. Through your marriage, you call them to the beautiful teachings of Islam.

Ahmad and Hamida have been married for almost fifty years. They have seven children and over fifteen grandchildren. Each child brought a unique test of learning how to raise them.

Ahmad and Hamida equally showed their care and concern for their children. They regularly ate dinner together as a family, prayed together, and spent their free time tending to their children's lives. It was important for them to provide their kids with a loving household where they knew their parents cared.

8. Read the Qur'ān together.

The Prophet ﷺ said, "No people gather to remember Allāh Mighty and Majestic but that the angels surround them, mercy envelopes them, tranquility descends upon them, and Allāh makes mention of them to those who are near Him." (*Muslim*, 2700)

- Read the Qur'ān in your house.
- Do a *khatm* together.
- Make *dhikr* and *ṣalāwāt* together.

Let the angels surround your household and bring blessings of mercy.

9. Learn together.

The Prophet ﷺ said, "Whoever travels a path in search of knowledge, Allāh will make easy for him a path to Paradise." (*Muslim*, 2699)

- Seek benefit together.
- Take Islamic courses together.
- Study together.

You could also take part in different classes, but study at similar times or share what you learned with each other.

10. Celebrate together.

The Prophet ﷺ said that Friday was of the best days, and in another narration he ﷺ said that Allāh granted Muslims the two Eid holidays as a replacement for other celebrations. (*Abū Dāwūd*, 1047 and 1134)

- Make certain times more special than others.
- Create a family tradition of celebrating Fridays and Eid together.
- Agree on how to best divide your time between family, friends, and yourselves.

Celebrate the favors of your Lord together.

Successful Muslim Couples form good habits for a lifetime. They cultivate their spirituality together and make their spiritual connection the forefront of their relationship.

SPIRITUAL CONNECTION

COUPLES EXERCISE

Agree on spiritual goals and family traditions as a couple. Discuss which acts of worship and rituals are important to you for the betterment of your marriage and family life.

Together

Choose a day and time that suits both of you. Find a relaxing place free of disruptions to attempt this exercise.

- Ask your spouse:
  - "Which acts of worship do you want to practice together?"
  - "Which family traditions are important to you?"
- Only one person should talk, while the other person listens.

For the spouse responding to the question:

- Do answer thoughtfully and from the heart.

  Inform your spouse how they can help you spiritually.

- Do not put down your spouse for not being as religious as you.

  Focus on helping them understand how important faith and family is to you.

For the spouse listening to the answer:

- Do act interested, give your spouse time to respond, and look at your spouse while they speak.
- Do not discourage your spouse's religious vigor or be judgmental of their family ideas.

Individually

After hearing what your spouse says, take some time to reflect on your conversation.

- Were you able to agree on good spiritual habits and family traditions? Why or why not?
- Do you share similar spiritual goals? Which ones are different?
- Do you share similar beliefs for family traditions? Which ones are different?

Be a Successful Muslim Couple

Love each other for the sake of Allāh. Focus on cultivating at least one spiritual goal or family tradition this week.

Reflections

SECRET #10

GROW TOGETHER

Yahya and Jessica were both reverts to Islam. They were from different cultural backgrounds, but they liked each other and decided to marry.

After their first child was born and with a second baby on the way, they decided to buy a house in a location that was better for their children.

Yahya exerted himself to gather the money to purchase their new home. It was spacious, comfortable, and everything Jessica wanted. They intended to live there for the rest of their lives.

Everything seemed perfect until Jessica fell into a disturbing state of sickness. Suddenly their world was turned upside down. Happy moments transformed into worrying agony.

Despite various medical interventions, they could not figure out how to fix her deteriorating state. The couple now struggled to deal with the challenging circumstances that surrounded their lives.

After many years of trying to make do with the situation, they decided to sell their home and move to a less reputable area.

Little did they know that this would be what Jessica needed. With a change in environment and new doctors, she was able to heal.

They never expected their lives to change so drastically, but what is more amazing is that their marital bond remained strong during the most testing of times. Even though they were hurting and doubting what the future held, they catered to each other's needs as best as they could and relied upon their faith to keep them strong.

Like all couples, Successful Muslim Couples go through hard times, disappointment, and uncertainty. Marriage is never a perfect story.

Successful Muslim Couples depend upon their spirituality to be the key source of their comfort and strength during trials. They remind each other to practice patience with their circumstances and to show gratitude for their blessings. Even within the toughest moments, they are a backbone and support for each other, growing together in their faith and love.

Most certainly, every problem in your marriage is an opportunity to become a better Muslim and a better spouse by way of your choices, your attitude, and your behavior.

It is important to not allow stressful situations to rip you apart. Life's trials can push you over the edge, which drives you to be less willing to restrain your emotions and watch your treatment of others.

However, being persistent in showing love despite your circumstances is what will pull you through the gloomy days. Most certainly, every problem in your marriage is an opportunity to become a better Muslim and a better spouse by way of your choices, your attitude, and your behavior.

The Prophet ﷺ said:

> **"Whoever helps ease one in difficulty, Allāh will make it easy for him in this world and the Hereafter."**

(*Muslim*, 2699)

Show up in the relationship through the thick and thin. Demonstrate your concern for your spouse's troubles and worries. The smallest act during the hardest times can bring the biggest benefit to your marriage.

Ask how your spouse is doing. Get them a cup of tea. Buy a sweet gift. Make them laugh.

Turn to Allāh together. Be a relief for each other. Use testing times as a reminder to appreciate your spouse's presence in your life.

The Prophet ﷺ depended on his wives during his most vulnerable moments.

When he ﷺ was scared for himself after receiving the first revelation, he ﷺ ran to Lady Khadīja ﵂ and took solace in her arms. (*Bukhārī*, 3)

When his sickness overtook him at the end of his life, he remained in Lady ʿĀʾisha's ﵂ living quarters and died in her arms. (*Bukhārī*, 4446)

The Prophet ﷺ started his mission and ended his mission in his spouse's arms.

Allāh Most High's words are true; spouses are garments for each other.

A Garment Protects.

Protect your spouse by fulfilling their needs and living up to your marital duties. Find out what are your spouse's most important needs.

Honor their requests as best as you can and show them every day that you really care. Prioritize your marital commitments. Do not let your things-to-do list come between your love.

A Garment Covers.

Cover each other's mistakes and weaknesses by forgiving sooner than later. Conflict doesn't have to break your marriage apart.

Seek to understand what happened, listen with compassion, empathize with your spouse's feelings, and forgive immediately.

Do not prolong the tension such that it begins to slowly tear your bond apart. Patch up any holes with extra love. Make your relationship a tranquil refuge.

A Garment Adorns.

Beautify your marriage with Prophetic character. The Prophet ﷺ is your role model of how to act and react in your marriage. The blessings in a marriage come from following his ﷺ beautiful ways.

Speak gently, smile frequently, laugh often, offer your loving support, and serve one another. Inspire each other towards goodness by the way you treat each other.

A Garment Holds Tightly.

Become one unit by connecting every day with a simple act of touch. Touch says what words cannot. Take care to send unlimited love messages to your spouse through hugs, kisses, holding hands, and the like.

Don't let go so soon. Hold on tight for as long as you can. Make tender touching a habit in your marriage.

A Garment Fits Just Right.

Mold your marriage into a lifelong friendship by being a dependable companion.

Your spouse is your other half. Together, you complete each other in the best of ways.

Let your presence be a source of comfort that quickly brings ease and joy to the other person's heart.

SPIRITUAL
CONNECTION

COUPLES EXERCISE

Find out what your spouse really thinks about your marriage. Brainstorm ways to improve your relationship and how to be a better support for each other.

Together

Choose a day and time that suits both of you. Find a relaxing place free of disruptions to attempt this exercise.

- ♥ Ask your spouse:
    - ✧ "Are you happy with our marriage?"
    - ✧ "How can our marriage be better?"
    - ✧ "What do you need from me during testing times?"
- ♥ Only one person should talk, while the other person listens.

For the spouse responding to the question:

- ♥ Do answer thoughtfully and from the heart. Let your spouse know how you feel about your marriage and your ideas of how the marriage can be better.
- ♥ Do not criticize your spouse for not being there for you in the past.

  Focus on helping them understand your needs, not putting them down for what they did wrong.

For the spouse listening to the answer:

- Do act interested, give your spouse time to respond, and look at your spouse while they speak.
- Do not get frustrated at your spouse's opinion or claim that they are exaggerating.

Individually

After hearing what your spouse says, take some time to reflect on your conversation.

- Are you both happy with your marriage? Why or why not?
- Were you able to agree on ways to improve your marital bond?
- Did you learn what your spouse needs during challenging times?

Be a Successful Muslim Couple

Be garments for each other. From the depths of your faith, be a pillar of support for your spouse during ease and hardship.

The Successful Muslim Couples Paradigm™

Heart Connection
Be devoted soulmates.

Emotional Connection
Be lifelong companions.

Physical Connection
Be passionate lovers.

Spiritual Connection
Be spiritual partners.

CONCLUDING THOUGHTS

UNHEALTHY SIGNS

After reading this book and attempting the exercises, you may be unsure about the state of your marriage. Perhaps you did not receive a positive response from your spouse, or you doubted whether your marriage could actually improve.

Unhealthy signs are red flags that alert you that your relationship may be in danger. However, they do not necessarily indicate that your marriage is doomed.

Rather they could signify that you both need to try harder to get out of bad habits or work with a qualified professional to guide you more appropriately for your specific situation.

Take note of any unhealthy signs in your marriage with the following list.

- ☐ You do not spend regular time with each other.
- ☐ You are not friends.
- ☐ You cannot share your thoughts, desires, and inner worlds with each other.
- ☐ You do not fulfill each other's core needs for love.
- ☐ You cannot discuss issues that bother you without it turning into a fight.
- ☐ You are not motivated to do nice things for each other.

- [ ] You put each other down and find it hard to appreciate each other.
- [ ] You are not willing to fulfill each other's sexual needs and desires.
- [ ] You do not support each other spiritually.
- [ ] Your relationship worsens during hard times.

⚠ If you checked more than two items, then you may want to consider third party support.

Seeking Help

Sometimes spouses are hesitant to seek third party support. They think that it will make their problems worse, or they are concerned about others knowing the details of their personal lives.

This is why it is important to carefully choose who you seek support from. The person who helps must be wise, have years of practical experience, and keep both spouses' best interests in mind.

Be cautious about relying on parents and family members to help you. Even though they may be good people, they may not be the best counselors. It is very difficult to remain fair when someone is your relative or friend.

Also, their advice may be limited because they do not have experience with a wider audience. What works for some relationships will not always work for others. So, their specific advice may not be what is needed for your situation.

The person who counsels your marriage must also have a good marriage too. Stay clear of friends and family members who willingly give advice, but they do not have any clue about what it takes to maintain a good marriage.

The best option in today's times is to find a counselor who you both feel comfortable with. This could be a community member, a scholar, or a professional in the field. Confirm that the counselor has a clear privacy policy and inquire about their procedure for helping couples.

Muslima Coaching offers professional marriage coaching for couples, wives, and singles. Please visit our website for more details at https://www.muslimacoaching.com. Our coaching options are:

- **Couples Coaching:** Work as a team to strengthen your relationship bond.
- **Wife Coaching:** Discover ideas of how to improve your marriage.
- **Premarital Coaching:** Learn about marriage and compatibility before you tie the knot.
- **Single Sisters Coaching:** Hear practical advice on how to choose the right spouse for you.

Further Reading

- The Seven Principles for Making a Marriage Work by John Gottman, PhD
- The Five Love Languages by Gary Chapman, PhD
- Men are from Mars, Women are from Venus by John Gray, PhD

ABOUT THE AUTHOR

All praise is due to Allāh, Lord of the Worlds.
May peace and blessings be upon His beloved Messenger ﷺ.

Naielah Ackbarali is the founder and CEO of Muslima Coaching. She studied various Islamic sciences with top traditional scholars in both Syria and Jordan for over 15 years. She is currently continuing her advanced Islamic studies in England.

Naielah is a trained strategic relationship coach, certified life coach, and a certified NLP Master Practitioner. Combined with her knowledge from Islamic studies, coaching experience, and personal marriage of more than 15 years, she offers faith-based marriage coaching to couples, wives, and singles.

She is an author of several books and has been featured on the Islam Channel and British Muslim TV.

Naielah has also written:

- "Secrets of Successful Muslim Wives" for all married sisters.
- "Say It With Love: Communicate, Connect & Cure Conflict" for all married sisters.
- "Love Scripts: Getting Through To Him" for all married sisters.
- "Newlywed Nuggets: Golden Marriage Advice" for newlywed wives.

- "A Muslim Woman's Guide To Menstruation Rulings" an intermediate guide for women ages 17+.
- "Fiqh of Menstruation Simplified: A Beginner's Guide for Muslim Women" for older teens, beginner learners, and converts.
- "Blossom: A Muslim Girl's Period Guide" for girls ages 9 to 14.
- "Ramadan Ready: Action Steps for Muslim Women" for older teens and all sisters.

She has produced free courses for sisters on fasting, umrah, and marriage. Find them on her website.

www.muslimacoaching.com
IG: @muslima_coaching FB: @muslimacoaching

Printed in Great Britain
by Amazon

46869284R00108